Homer

A Transitional Reader

ANCIENT GREEK TRANSITIONAL READER SERIES

The **Ancient Greek Transitional Reader Series** took its inspiration from the LEGAMUS Transitional Reader Series, a Latin reader series created and coedited by Kenneth F. Kitchell Jr. (University of Massachusetts Amherst) and Thomas Sienkewicz (Monmouth College). Like that series, the intention behind the Ancient Greek Transitional Reader Series is to facilitate reading above all else.

The series is designed to address the difficulties that confront intermediate college and high school students moving from adapted Greek texts in introductory courses to reading unadapted Greek. Volumes in the series can be used both individually, as an introduction to a single author, or in combination, to form a survey reading course that gives students first exposure to a variety of authors.

Homer

A Transitional Reader

John H. O'Neil and Timothy F. Winters

Bolchazy-Carducci Publishers, Inc.

Mundelein, Illinois USA

Volume Editor: Timothy Beck
Contributing Editors: Laurel Draper and Laurie Haight Keenan
Cover Design & Typography: Adam Phillip Velez

Homer
A Transitional Reader

John H. O'Neil and Timothy F. Winters

Bolchazy-Carducci Publishers, Inc.
1570 Baskin Road
Mundelein, Illinois 60060
www.bolchazy.com

Printed in the United States of America
2016
by Publishers' Graphics

ISBN 978-0-86516-720-9

Library of Congress Cataloging-in-Publication Data

O'Neil, John H.
  Homer : a transitional reader / John H. O'Neil and Timothy F. Winters.
    p. cm. -- (Ancient Greek transitional reader series)
  Commentary in English with selections from Homer in Greek.
  Selections from Homer's Iliad, each selection with vocabulary and grammar notes, exercises, and a grammar review.
  ISBN 978-0-86516-720-9 (pbk. : alk. paper) 1. Greek language--Readers. 2. Greek language--Grammar--Problems,
exercises, etc. I. Winters, Timothy F. II. Homer. Iliad. Selections. 2010 III. Title.
  PA260.O64 2010
  883'.01--dc22
                                                                                    2010040083

CONTENTS

PREFACE

How to Use This Reader

Among the true literary classics throughout history are several that readers continue to approach with awe, both because of their genuine uniqueness in artistry and because their reputations are widely known. In this class of works are the two epic poems traditionally ascribed to Homer, the *Iliad* and the *Odyssey*. It is our goal in this text to make the timeless story of Achilles' anger available and accessible to students on an intermediate level, in the Greek in which it was recorded.

In the readings that follow, you will encounter Greek of a different sort from that to which you are accustomed. Both the story and the great part of the composition of these poems were remote from classical Athens not only in distance but also in time. A large number of variant word forms will appear interspersed with forms familiar to you from Attic Greek. These variants in most cases represent several dialects, or regional branches of the language, and often also betray the general time frame within which they entered the story.

Dialectic variation comprises one of the greatest challenges to a student beginning to read Homeric Greek for the first time. This text provides extensive help in learning to recognize the common variants. Read the sections on dialect thoroughly and carefully, as they will be applicable toward all of the readings, and toward any additional reading in Greek epic that you may do in the future.

In addition to helpful discussions about dialect, this text provides other supportive features. If you utilize these appropriately, you will soon find that you are quickly gaining proficiency in reading and comprehension. We strongly suggest that the teacher and the student work through each reading in the sequence as presented, from the summary through the grammatical review and practice exercises, on to the pre-reading encounter with the text and its notes, the questions for thought as you read, and finally the passage as it appears in the *Iliad*, along with accompanying notes and vocabulary, and the questions for thought following the reading. This sequence is intended to provide optimal review of grammatical constructions and significant forms, and expansion and retention of vocabulary, as well as a smooth transition from the pre-reading to the full reading of each passage. To omit any of the material in an attempt to reach the full passage would defeat the goal.

Our approach to the authorship of the *Iliad* deserves brief explanation. As is noted in several places in this textbook, there has long been confusion as to whether an individual named "Homer" existed, and if so whether that individual was the authentic creator of the works attributed to him. Although we have in the course of this book for the most part followed the convention of referring to "Homer," we have tried not to lead students consciously or inadvertently into a particular set of assumptions regarding this question. The teacher and the student should bear in mind however that the question of authorship is very complex, and alternate views must be entertained.

The pre-reading in each chapter is an altered version of the text. Poetic contractions and metrical elisions have been restored, and in some instances irregularities in word forms have been glossed. The pre-reading stage is accompanied by grammatical notes. The unaltered reading, which falls near the end of each chapter, is supported with notes aiming toward the student's appreciation of the poetry through an understanding of meter, literary figures of speech, and pertinent cultural background information. In the course of these notes the student is often referred to the supplemental materials, which include an explanatory section on dactylic hexameter (pages xviii–xix), an alphabetical listing of common figures of speech with definitions and examples (pages 108–113), and an index of proper names (pages 114–115) intended to provide a fuller understanding of both the places mentioned and the role of the characters. The student is urged to make frequent use of these aids.

Each unaltered reading is also accompanied by a list of vocabulary found within the given reading but not commonplace throughout the epic. Frequent use of the general vocabulary at the end of the book is to be expected in the early readings. Note that if a word does not appear in the list alongside the reading, and must be located in the general vocabulary, the word should be considered as one appearing with frequency throughout Homeric poetry. Students are encouraged to create and maintain their own vocabulary lists or flashcards in order to learn these words precisely and quickly. Students who create such a personalized list will notice that before too many readings have passed they are making fewer visits to the general vocabulary. This level of comfort with the vocabulary will be one signal that students are well on the way to reading the Greek of Homer.

ACKNOWLEDGMENTS

As is true in the case of any project resulting in a book, the authors owe thanks to a number of persons. We would like to acknowledge our families, our colleagues, and our students, many of whom were patient enough to help us work through early drafts of the chapters in a classroom setting. Their comments were extremely helpful. Our gratitude is extended to Tim Beck and to Bridget Buchholz for their close and precise editorial work. We also wish to acknowledge Bolchazy-Carducci, Publishers; Laurie Haight Keenan, Senior Editor; and in particular Thomas Sienkewicz and Kenneth Kitchell, by whose vision through their conception of the *Legamus* series the powerful literature of the Romans, and now the Greeks, can be made accessible to intermediate students in a systematic program.

And now, *legamus*; let's read!

JHO   TFW

INTRODUCTION TO HOMER

The *Iliad* As a Literary Phenomenon

The Homeric poems evolved over a long period of time, and were finally recorded considerably later than the dimly remembered events they narrate. This intriguing fact poses challenges for the reader. Anachronisms, inconsistencies in dialects within the same poem (or even within a given line of poetry), and the mystery of how much or how little the actual words in the poems changed over time represent just a few of these hurdles. For example, archaeological evidence is at odds with the epics' descriptions of ship construction: the poems do not reflect methods in evidence at the end of the Mycenaean Bronze Age (*ca.* 1200–1100 BCE), by scholarly consensus the period of the Trojan War. As to dialect, note that the root of the name Achilles, the *Iliad*'s central character, appears in no less than three variants. It is fair to say that the *Iliad* and the *Odyssey*, during the period of their evolution into full-scale poems with integrity of plot, sequence, and character development, were analogous to living and growing organisms, rather than rigid and frozen in time, until ultimately they were written down.

Given that our subject is so fluid, then, two very knotty questions must be addressed before one should launch into a survey of passages from the *Iliad*. First, we need some sense of how the poetry in its oral phase might have been received by an audience. Then, we have to understand something of the complex journey of the poetry—from its inception amid the legends of Troy, to that point at which it was *written* in more or less its present form.

Entertaining the House: An Exercise in Versatility

You have a general sense of how the Homeric epics were imparted to an audience if you have read any portions of *Beowulf*. The scops would recite sections of the long tale, each performer no doubt gaining a popular following, and developing what would become favorite scenes and vignettes, or "little pictures," from within the larger story. Scholars believe that these scops possessed a vast memory-storehouse of legendary and historical material, and that they drew on certain metrical words or phrases, called *formulae*, to express typical or characteristic action, or as descriptors of persons or places. The structure and meter of the poetic line and, of course, the language of the *Beowulf* poet or poets were significantly different from those of the Homeric epics; but in essence the creative—or properly speaking *re*-creative—processes were very similar.

Such a mode of entertainment is difficult for us to imagine; we today have very different cultural norms and different vehicles to preserve our facts, legends, and lore—not to mention to while away dark evenings. But try to recall whether you have ever listened to a musician singing a folk song or ballad while strumming a guitar. In principle, this is the same practice. A modern musician touring different venues often varies the program either slightly or significantly, adapting the songs to the particular audience, at times even altering the text of a song to achieve a certain effect or elicit a certain response, while other elements of the song remain constant among all audiences. A story or series of stories about human experience is told or retold. The descriptive language of the ballad incites in the imagination vivid pictures of action and character, and so evokes an emotional response. The hearer maintains and strengthens connections to a heritage whose origins may well be in the distant past. Thoughts and emotions common to all peoples are validated, and we are reminded of our present-day connectedness to other people. This process is in essence identical to the delivery of ancient epic poetry.

TWO TALES OF A CITY: CALVERT, SCHLIEMANN AND THE DISCOVERY OF TROY

The story about our discovery of the true nature of the Homeric poems may be likened to a traveler's toilsome journey through rugged terrain. It is a saga as dynamic, serpentine, and protean as the epics themselves. In "modern-day" terms, it began in the early 1800s, when concern with Homer and ancient epic poetry did not enjoy general popularity. Most scholars of that time assumed on the one hand that Homer was historically an early Greek poet who had composed, possibly among other works, two long epics whose premises stemmed from the siege of Troy; and on the other hand that the events and characters in the stories, and Troy itself, were merely the stuff of fantasy.

Some individuals, however, took a different view. In 1822, a Scottish editor, Charles Maclaren, while boasting no formal education or training, not only proposed that Homer's Troy had been a historical place, but also hazarded a guess at a possible location. Subsequently, a reserved young diplomat, Frank Calvert, would confirm Maclaren's intuition. Calvert lived in Turkey, where he supported the diplomatic careers of his more outgoing brothers by composing many of the requisite letters sent out of their offices. In 1847, one of his brothers bought a parcel of land in northwest Turkey, which included part of a hill known as Hisarlik—the location that Maclaren had proposed as the site of ancient Troy. Having begun cautious excavations, Calvert became convinced that the site was authentic. But, though connected to the diplomatic echelons, he could not secure funding to launch exhaustive explorations. Here, fate intervened. Calvert posed his dilemma to Heinrich Schliemann, an enterprising cosmopolite who shared Calvert's zeal and conviction about Troy. Schliemann afforded the funding to expand Calvert's initial work at Hisarlik on into the 1870s. At a point, however, deep complications arose in the relationship. Whereas Frank Calvert was in a professional position to acquire many of the permits necessary to carry out their work, and was possessed of an innate sense of the delicacy of the archaeological process (at a time when archaeology was not yet a scientific and systematic discipline), all the same, Schliemann's funds seem to have carried more weight. The patron largely appropriated the project, and as far as subsequent history is concerned, appropriated along with it the credit for Troy's discovery.

In his haste to reveal to the world the layer of ground beneath Hisarlik where he believed the Iliadic Troy lay, Schliemann actually destroyed much of what he was looking for. Subsequent evidence, culled from Schliemann's own journal and from the work of later scholars, indicates further that he hoarded artifacts he found, smuggled many out of Turkey illegally, and fabricated details surrounding the discovery of a quantity of items. He has even been indicted as having had fake artifacts produced. Impulsive and romantic by nature, Schliemann was prone to decree the provenance of artifacts upon sight: he notoriously "identified" the Treasure of Helen, and had his wife Sophia photographed while dressed in the regalia. Calvert objected to Schliemann's methods, but the original excavator's own tragic flaws were his soft temperament and his financial need.

Out of this complex entanglement, two undeniable facts emerge. The first is that, whatever their personal motivations and interpersonal disagreements, Calvert and Schliemann contributed an extremely high-profile specimen to the fledgling discipline of archaeology, setting the stage for later significant work at Hisarlik (1932–38) by Dr. Carl Blegen of the University of Cincinnati. The second undeniable fact is that, however controversial and dubious some chapters of their story may seem, the common conviction of Maclaren, Calvert, and Schliemann brought about a quantum advancement in Homeric studies, altering for all time how the epics are to be read.

DID THE STONES SING? ARCHAEOLOGICAL EVIDENCE OF EARLY GREEK WRITING

Whether Homeric literature as we have it preserves a stage in a shifting oral transmission, or is the work of a single poet, or something between, the Mycenaean culture (*ca.* 1600–1100 BCE) that these poems dimly reflect was not illiterate. In the late nineteenth century, harbingers of latent Bronze Age scripts had caught the eye of Sir Arthur Evans, an English scholar with a passion for archaeology. While visiting the island of Crete, he had taken note of certain charms, decorated with distinct characters, frequently worn by local women. In the spring of 1900, Evans discovered a cache of clay tablets bearing similar characters while excavating the palace at Cnossos, on Crete. In time, the quantity of similar evidence would increase with additional discoveries throughout mainland Greece and elsewhere. Evans assumed the Cnossos site to be the palace of the fabled Cretan ruler, Minos, and so named the entire lost culture "Minoan." The tablets he had found proved to bear three different scripts. Two of them yet remain undeciphered; the third, however, began to yield its secrets before just a few decades had passed. This script, called Linear B, dated generally to around 1500 BCE, would provide a *written* link to the Bronze Age of Troy and Mycenae.

During the early 1940s, Alice Kober, a young classicist at Brooklyn College, set about attempting to break the silence of the Cnossos tablets. Picking up on the trail of Evans, who had been thwarted in the same desire, Kober noticed that elements of the Linear B script appeared to contain common word roots and what seemed to have been case endings. She inferred a relationship with Greek, a link that Evans had disavowed. Kober died before attaining her goal. It has been discovered only recently how significant was the debt owed her by her colleagues—American Professor Emmett Bennett, who devised the organizational system for the ninety characters in the script, and Britons Michael Ventris and John Chadwick, who ultimately were credited with deciphering the code between 1951 and 1953 and confirming it as a Mycenaean Greek script.

A somewhat celebrated example illustrating the link between Greek and Linear B is the appearance in Linear B of the phrase *TO-SA PA-KA-NA*, or τόσα φάσγανα, "so many swords." The noun φάσγανον is not incidental in the epics: it appears nineteen times in the *Iliad*, and six in the *Odyssey*. The revelation that an element of Mycenaean Greek culture inhabited Crete at some distant time was significant. Furthermore, the indication of a flashpoint of commonality between the vocabulary and grammar of the epics and the Linear B tablets honed the question of the degree of Bronze Age material preserved in the oral tradition. The surviving clay tablets seemingly contained itemized records and government documents; there long seemed to be no clear traces in them of *literary* activity, beyond the numerous recognizable names and epithets of familiar deities. But in recent years a scholar has noticed intriguing patterns in the tablets, such as section headings that clearly indicate a conscious meter. One particular specimen falls naturally into dactylic hexameter, and displays both multiple elisions and a caesura (see Introduction to Meter, p. xviii). The famous Phaistos Disk, dated as early as 2000 to 1500 BCE (presuming it is authentic), has suggested to the eye of another scholar a structured pattern of repeated and unrepeated words—as yet untranslatable—suggestive of the introduction of a song, followed by antiphonal parts, or "calls" and "responses." Such observations offer exciting hints that literary composition in some degree may well have been afoot and acknowledged as an artistic pursuit in an earlier era than has traditionally been accepted. The quest to discover fully the meaning and significance contained in these treasures of clay continues, with the hope of gleaning further understanding of the Mycenaean mind and the extent of its artistic creativity.

WRITTEN ON THE WIND? SCHOLARS TRY TO DETERMINE HOW THE EPICS WERE COMPOSED

Once the existence of Troy had been confirmed, Homeric scholarship was beset with countless new questions, and myriad new ways of looking at the languages and artifacts of a time so distant that it had previously been considered mythical. The question of authorship of the Homeric epics and the methods of their composition rose to the level of extended and informed debate, involving explorations in fields from archaeology to philology. A vast body of work was undertaken by a growing cadre of scholars, many of them American.

Less than sixty years after the work at Troy began in earnest, Homeric scholarship took another leap. The theories of a young scholar incited what became known as "The Homeric Question," the issue of the manner of composition and authorship of the epics. In the 1920s, while barely twenty years old, Milman Parry, an American graduate student at the University of Paris, had already begun to publish his observations regarding the Homeric poems. He illustrated convincingly that many phrases are used repeatedly in both the *Iliad* and the *Odyssey*. These phrases, called *formulae* (as in *Beowulf*), are metrical units, often found in the same metrical location in their respective lines of the epics. This pattern suggested to Parry that something unusual had been at work in the composition of the poems—that they in effect had enjoyed lives of their own as orally transmitted tradition, as a mode of preserving not only story, but also cultural customs and ideals in a time prior to the capacity to record these in written form. Simply stated, Parry's conclusions suggest multiple generations of "authors," building and enhancing a highly efficient system of oral poetry. Supposing that the *formulae* served as memory aids as well as compositional building blocks, Parry reasoned that improvisation may have constantly shaped the retelling of the events associated with the Trojan War. Changes over time, both insignificant and substantive, might have occurred. Parry inferred that in addition to *formulae*, elements such as characters and plot were inherited from previous generations of epic poets. Yet despite any inherited elements, the very nature of oral transmission and the re-creative process that Parry envisioned provided the bards a wide field for innovation.

The young Parry was recommended to a scholar of oral epic stories preserved in Balkan culture. Parry had been given an advantage hardly imaginable: an accessible test case for his theory about the Homeric epics. Between 1933 and 1935, Parry, now a professor at Harvard University, twice traveled to Bosnia to study and to record traditional epic songs. Just as the published documentation of his work and his articulation of the theory of oral composition were beginning in their own way to revolutionize Homeric studies, Parry himself died. His son Adam subsequently edited and published his remaining papers. Milman Parry's work was also carried on by his assistant and colleague at Harvard, Albert Lord, who continued to investigate the Bosnian oral traditions, and expanded his inquiries into other early epics of various cultures, including the Sumerian *Epic of Gilgamesh*, the French *Song of Roland*, and the Anglo-Saxon *Beowulf*. In each, the telltale elements of oral composition were evident.

The use of inherited themes and language in no way diminishes the role of the individual singer. A single, highly accomplished poet might have composed one or both epics by imposing form on a relatively unstructured mass of oral tradition. Cedric H. Whitman, also of Harvard, insisted that the structure of each the *Iliad* and the *Odyssey* could only have been conceived by one poet with one unified purpose. He argued that elements of plot—characters, events, motifs—formed geometrical patterns within the progression of a poem, with one event later echoed, or balanced, by a similar event told in a similar style. The overall impression that results from close inspection of the poems is of a meticulous overlaying of symmetry, and a complex interweaving of images, actions, and personalities. It follows that the high degree of structure evident in the poems provided support for the memory of an oral poet, similar to the way *formulae* might have prompted a storyteller. At some point, then, one poet might have amassed a large reservoir of oral tradition, and set himself about crafting unified poems with rare artistry.

GET IT IN WRITING: THE EPICS RECORDED

Theories about when, where, and why the orally conceived epics were committed to writing are numerous and troublesome. Some look to a presumed urgency that a "canonical" text be captured. While it was common practice for bards to sing at major festivals throughout Greece, were the *Iliad* to have been presented as a unified work in such a setting it would have required three days or more to recite—a strain on mortal vocal chords, though a relay team of singers may have kept the tale going. As numerous singers handled the storytelling, and the risk increased that nuances of plot and character and the unity of the composition would suffer corruption, a master poet may have safeguarded the creations in written "master" copies, or dictated them to scribes. There is some support for the suggestion that the purposeful gathering and ordering of loose segments of the sagas took place at the command of the Athenian tyrant Pisistratus, at some point after the mid-sixth century BCE, coinciding with his reported institution or revitalization of the Panathenean Festival. Such a hypothesis may account for some of the Attic dialect forms that appear in narratives far removed from Athens. At the same time, it should be noted that Homeric poetry admits a range of non-Attic dialect forms inherited, presumably, from the centuries-long development and synthesis of oral poetics over time and in various communities.

One further example will serve to indicate the difficulties encountered in establishing a date for the written recording of the epics. It has been argued that the very name of an individual "Homer" is a later imposition on the Homeric tradition, with some focus on the "Homeridai"—a guild of rhapsodes attested from the fifth century BCE that performed works about gods and heroes, including the *Iliad* and the *Odyssey*. One prominent scholar of early Greek poetry, Martin L. West, has recently suggested the group's name could have grown from roots meaning, "an assembly singing together," with the implication that the name "Homer" was then artificially and subsequently derived from "Homeridai"—interpreted to mean "sons of Homer"—and assigned to an assumed composer of the early poems.

Such is the complexity in tracing the evolution of these epic tales, which emerged from an anonymous oral tradition to become no less than primary textbooks for the pupils of Greek antiquity, and which to this day compel study and admiration.

THE STORY AND THE STUDY GO ON

After more than two centuries of modern scholarship, as one discovery after another has pointed to the poetry's oral composition while a similar drama has played out in defining the very concept of its "authorship," the "Homeric Question" remains. What evidence lies concealed? Who will make the discoveries, notice the pattern, decipher the unknown script, trace the fateful word? Will *you*? The answers may continue to be as elusive of our grasp as the shades in the Underworld. But the controversies, the mysteries, the compulsion for us to have a final answer, need not and should not diminish our wonder at and appreciation of the breadth and depth of human experience preserved in Greek epic.

SUGGESTED FURTHER READING

Allen, Susan Heuck. 1999. *Finding the Walls of Troy: Frank Calvert and Heinrich Schliemann at Hisarlik.* Berkeley.

Chadwick, John. 1990. *The Decipherment of Linear B.* 2nd ed. Cambridge, UK.

Fowler, R., ed. 2004. *The Cambridge Companion to Homer.* Cambridge, UK.

Lord, Albert B. 2000. *The Singer of Tales.* 2nd ed. Edited by Stephan Mitchell and Gregory Nagy. Cambridge, MA.

Morris, Ian and Barry Powell, eds. 1997. *A New Companion to Homer.* Leiden.

Nagy, Gregory. 1998. *The Best of the Achaeans: Concepts of the Hero in Archaic Greek Poetry.* Rev. ed. Baltimore.

Page, Denys. 1959. *History and the Homeric* Iliad. Berkeley.

Parry, Adam, ed. 1987. *The Making of Homeric Verse: The Collected Papers of Milman Parry.* New York.

Powell, Barry B. 2004. *Homer.* Blackwell Introductions to the Classical World. Malden, MA.

Shay, Jonathan. 1994. *Achilles in Vietnam: Combat Trauma and the Undoing of Character.* New York.

———. 2002. *Odysseus in America: Combat Trauma and the Trials of Homecoming.* New York.

Taplin, Oliver. 1992. *Homeric Soundings: The Shaping of the* ILIAD. Oxford.

West, Martin L. 1982. *Greek Metre.* Oxford.

———. 1999. "The Invention of Homer." *The Classical Quarterly*, New Series, Vol. 49: 364–82.

Whitman, Cedric H. 1967. *Homer and the Heroic Tradition.* Cambridge, MA.

Younger, John. 2007. "The Aegean Bard: Evidence for Sound and Song." In *EPOS: Reconsidering Greek Epic and Aegean Bronze Age Archaeology*, edited by S. Morris and R. Laffineur, pp. 71–78. Liège and Austin.

INTRODUCTION TO METER

Dactylic Hexameter

Dactylic hexameter is the meter in which epic poetry, along with other genres, was composed in the ancient Greco-Roman world, and indeed some modern poets have also used it—though many would say that dactylic hexameter does not work well in the English language.

Hold your left index finger horizontally in front of your eyes. What you see is one long section, followed by two short—the metric foundation of the dactylic hexameter. The word δάκτυλος in Greek means finger, and a dactyl is just that, one long syllable followed by two short syllables. In any **dactyl**, the two short syllables can be replaced by one long, a configuration called a **spondee**. Dactylic hexameter is a scheme that employs six metrical feet, each composed of one dactyl or one spondee.

The long and short syllables of Greek meter were quantitative, that is, they were a measure of the quantity of time it took to pronounce the vowel. **Scansion** is the marking of these long and short syllables, along with natural breaks in the line. Such a break generally occurs toward the middle of a line and is called a **caesura.** A caesura generally occurs in the third or fourth foot, but can occur earlier or later. The final syllable may scan as either long or short.

In the first line of the *Iliad*, the end of the word Πηληϊάδεω displays a condition known as **synizesis,** in which two vowels that normally do not form a diphthong must be pronounced as a single syllable.

Two more peculiarities of Greek meter should be mentioned. **Hiatus** occurs when a vowel at word-end that is usually elided before a subsequent initial vowel must instead be pronounced. An example in English would be "the egg." The stop that occurs creates an unpleasant break. Hiatus frequently reflects the preservation of traditional language pre-dating later developments, such as the loss of a "w" sound that once appeared between the two vowels at the beginning of the second word. Finally, **epic correption** is a particular form of hiatus in which a long vowel at word-end must be read as short when followed by a vowel at the beginning of the next word. You will see each form of hiatus in the readings often.

Here is the opening of the *Iliad* with the lines marked for scansion.

$$\text{–}\ \cup\ \cup\ \text{–}\ \cup\ \cup\ \text{–}\ \qquad \text{–}\ \text{–}\cup\cup\ \text{–}\ \cup\ \cup\ \text{–}\ \times$$

μῆνιν ἄειδε, θεά, ‖ Πηληϊάδεω Ἀχιλῆος

$$\text{–}\ \cup\ \cup\ \text{–}\ \qquad \text{–}\ \text{–}\ \cup\ \cup\ \text{–}\ \text{–}\ \text{–}\ \cup\ \cup\ \text{–}\ \times$$

οὐλομένην, ‖ ἣ μυρί᾽ Ἀχαιοῖς ἄλγε᾽ ἔθηκε,

$$\text{–}\ \text{–}\ \text{–}\ \text{–}\ \text{–}\ \text{–}\ \cup\cup\ \text{–}\ \cup\cup\text{–}\ \times$$

πολλὰς δ᾽ ἰφθίμους ψυχὰς ‖ Ἄϊδι προΐαψεν

$$\text{–}\ \text{–}\ \text{–}\ \qquad \text{–}\ \text{–}\ \cup\ \cup\ \text{–}\ \cup\cup\ \text{–}\ \cup\ \cup\ \text{–}\ \times$$

ἡρώων, ‖ αὐτοὺς δὲ ἑλώρια τεῦχε κύνεσσιν

5   οἰωνοῖσί τε πᾶσι, ‖ Διὸς δ᾽ ἐτελείετο βουλή,

ἐξ οὗ δὴ τὰ πρῶτα ‖ διαστήτην ἐρίσαντε

Ἀτρεΐδης τε ἄναξ ἀνδρῶν ‖ καὶ δῖος Ἀχιλλεύς.

In the first line, there is a natural pause (‖) following the word θεά. In the second line that pause occurs a bit earlier, just after οὐλομένην. Homer sometimes manipulates these pauses to great effect. For example in line 1, by pausing where he does, the poet allows Achilles' epithet and name to fill the last part of the line, giving it more emphasis, more punch. Again, by pausing after οὐλομένην in line two, the listener is invited to think about that word for just a moment longer.

As you read through the poem, make it a practice to write out the scansion of the first five lines of each reading to become comfortable with the process. As you become proficient at scansion, and discover how the poet manipulates meter and pauses, your appreciation of the poem will deepen.

LIST OF ABBREVIATIONS

act.	active	interr.	interrogative
acc.	accusative	lit.	literally
adj.	adjective	mid.	middle
adv.	adverb	neut.	neuter
aor.	aorist	obj.	object
attrib.	attributive	opt.	optative
cf.	compare, *confer*, "consult"	partit.	partitive
circumst.	circumstantial	pass.	passive
compar.	comparative	pf.	perfect
condit.	conditional	pl.	plural
dir. obj.	direct object	possess.	possessive
e.g.	*exempli gratia*, "for example"	pple.	participle
esp.	especially	prep.	preposition
fem.	feminine	pron.	pronoun
fut.	future	rel.	relative
i.e.	namely, *id est*, "that is (I mean)"	reflex.	reflexive
imperat.	imperative	sc.	*scilicet*, "(it is permitted to) understand"
impers.	impersonal	sing.	singular
impf.	imperfect	superl.	superlative
indic.	indicative	subj.	subject
indir.	indirect	subjnc.	subjunctive
infin.	infinitive		

READING 1

Homer States the Theme and Introduces the Two Principal Figures

(Iliad 1.1–7)

BEFORE YOU READ WHAT HOMER COMPOSED

Introduction

Epics begin *in medias res* ("in the middle of things"), but in the opening lines the audience is oriented to the events to be narrated. Thus the opening **proem** of Homer's *Iliad* states the destructive anger of Achilles as the theme of the poem and signals the identity of the principal characters. We hear that the gods are intimately involved in the story's events, as the "will of Zeus was fulfilled." And the gods will be involved in telling the story itself—the proem (lines 1–7) is an extended prayer to a Muse (θεά), daughter of Memory and Zeus, who breathes inspiration directly into poets.

Being a sensitive reader requires an awareness of the differences and similarities in worldview between one's own culture and experience and that of the author. To get a sense of the cultural context, watch how the poem's characters respond to their emotions, how they interact with the gods and one another, and how they come to a deeper understanding of their place in the world.

With a little preparation, you will soon be reading the text of Homer and the story of Achilles' wrath.

Keep This Grammar in Mind — PARTICIPLES

A participle is a verbal adjective. It has some characteristics of verbs (tense and voice), and some of adjectives (case, number, and gender). English verbs have only two participles, one that indicates continuous action and one for completed action. These participles function as adjectives in phrases such as "the (continuously) speaking man," or "the (completely) spoken word."

While participles are widely used in English, they are even more common in Greek. A full Greek verb has twelve participles and, compared to English, these offer a Greek speaker more flexibility. There are active, middle, and passive participles for four tenses: present, future, aorist, and perfect.

Keep in mind the following:

- The **aorist** shows simply that the action took place once and was finished, e.g., "I ate."
- The **perfect** shows that the action took place in the past but continues to have an effect on the present; this may require the addition of a brief phrase to your translation to show the participle's full force, e.g., "I have eaten *and so I am not hungry now.*"
- Likewise, it may be necessary to add a brief phrase to show the force of the **middle voice,** e.g., "having destroyed the letters *out of self-interest,* he returned to Greece."

The same principles used to recognize the tense of conjugated Greek verbs also apply to participles. For example:

- **Future** participles of regular verbs are marked by a sigma, as in λύ-**σ**-ων.
- **Aorist** active and middle participles regularly have a sigma-alpha pattern, as in λῦ-**σα**-ς.
- **Perfect** participles show reduplication, as in **λε**-λυ-κώς.

Work on mastering the various participles. You will increase your reading speed if you can recognize and quickly determine a participle's function in a particular line.

	Active	Middle	Passive
Present	λύων, -ουσα, -ον destroying	λυόμενος, -η, -ον destroying	λυόμενος, -η, -ον (being) destroyed
Future	λύσων, -σουσα, -σον going to destroy	λυσόμενος, -η, -ον going to destroy	λυθησόμενος, -η, -ον going to be destroyed
Aorist	λύσας, -σασα, -σαν having destroyed	λυσάμενος, -η, -ον having destroyed	λυθείς, -θεῖσα, -θέν having been destroyed
Perfect	λελυκώς, -κυῖα, -κόν having destroyed	λελυμένος, -η, -ον having destroyed	λελυμένος, -η, -ον having been destroyed

In both the present and perfect tense, middle and passive participles are identical in form. Note also that seven of the eight middle/passive participles share the same ending, **-μενος, -η, -ον.**

Stopping for Some Practice — PARTICIPLES

Participles are among the most common verb forms in Greek literature. The following occur in this reading:

οὐλομένην, "destroying, destructive" from ὄλλυμι, "destroy"

ἐρίσαντε, "quarreling" from ἐρίζω, "contend, dispute, quarrel"

χολωθείς, "angered" from χολόω, "be angry."

In the space provided, list the tense, voice, case, number, and gender for each participle, and then translate into English. All will appear in this reading and the next. The unusual dual participle ἐρίσαντε is provided as an example.

	Tense	Voice	Case	Number	Gender	Translation
ἐρίσαντε	aorist	active	nominative	dual	masculine	"the two (men) quarreling"
οὐλομένην	_____	_____	_____	_____	_____	_____
χολωθείς	_____	_____	_____	_____	_____	_____
λυσόμενος	_____	_____	_____	_____	_____	_____
φέρων	_____	_____	_____	_____	_____	_____

Stopping for Some Practice — NOUN / ADJECTIVE AGREEMENT

The following nouns and adjectives appear in the first reading. Match each noun with the correct adjective. You may use the vocabulary in Appendix C (pp. 116–22) to check a noun's gender.

1. _____ Ἀχιλλεύς   A. μυρία

2. _____ μῆνιν   B. ἰφθίμους

3. _____ οἰωνοῖσι   C. δῖος

4. _____ ἄλγεα   D. πᾶσι

5. _____ ψυχάς   E. οὐλομένην

HELPING YOU READ WHAT HOMER COMPOSED

Vocabulary

ἀείδω, ἀείσομαι, ἄεισα, sing

Ἀΐδης, -αο, ὁ, Hades, i.e., the Underworld

ἄλγος, -εος, τό, pain, distress

Ἀτρεΐδης, -αο, ὁ, son of Atreus, i.e., Agamemnon

Ἀχαιοί, -ῶν, οἱ, Achaeans

Ἀχιλ(λ)εύς, -ῆος, ὁ, Achilles

δϊΐστημι, διαστήσω, διέστησα / διέστην, διέστηκα, stand apart

ἕλωρ, —, τό, spoil, prey

ἐρίζω, —, ἔρισα, quarrel

Ζεύς, Διός, ὁ, Zeus

ἴφθιμος, -ον, strong

μῆνις, -ιος, ἡ, wrath, ire

οἰωνός, -οῦ, ὁ, bird

οὐλόμενος, -η, -ον, destroying, destructive

Πηληϊάδης, -εω, ὁ, son of Peleus

προϊάπτω, προϊάψω, προΐαψα, throw, hurl

Notes

1   μῆνιν: dir. obj. of ἄειδε; a small group of nouns have acc. sing. -ιν, e.g., πόλις

   Πηληϊάδεω: gen. with Ἀχιλῆος; masc. 1st declen. nouns regularly show Homeric gen. sing. in -αο / -εω. Keep in mind that an Index of Significant Names can be found in Appendix B (pp. 114–15).

   Ἀχιλῆος: Attic = Ἀχιλέως; the 3rd declen. gen. sing. ending is easier to identify before the vowel quantities shift in Attic

2   οὐλομένην: with μῆνιν; Homeric diction has access to the (Aeolic) metrical variation -ου- for Attic -ο-

   ἥ: rel. pron. referring to μῆνιν; subj. of ἔθηκε, προΐαψεν, and τεῦχε

   ἄλγεα: originally ἄλγεσα, Attic = τὰ ἄλγη; uncontracted 3rd declen. sigma-stem endings are easier to identify than their contracted Attic forms

   ἔθηκε: aor. < τίθημι, "that put . . . "

3   ἰφθίμους: fem. acc. pl., with ψυχάς; adjs. of two terminations use no distinctly fem. endings

   Ἀΐδι: three-syllable epic variant of Ἅδης; dat. shows movement toward a place of rest, "unto Hades"

4   ἑλώρια: appositive with αὐτούς, "[Achilles' anger] made *them* into *prey*"

   τεῦχε: impf.; augments are freely absent in Homeric Greek, allowing for metrical variation

   κύνεσσιν: Attic = κύνεσι(ν); this 3rd declen. dat. pl. offers a metrical alternative

4–5   κύνεσσιν / οἰωνοῖσί τε πᾶσι: "for all the dogs and birds"

5   οἰωνοῖσι: Attic = οἰωνοῖς; be alert for this common metrical alternative to the 2nd declen. dat. pl.

   Διός: gen. sing., dependent on βουλή

   ἐτελείετο: impf. pass. < τελέω

6   ἐξ οὗ: referring to the time of the incident that sparked Achilles' anger

   τὰ πρῶτα: adv., "(when) first"

   διαστήτην: dual aor., "the two of them stood apart"; unaugmented forms are common

   ἐρίσαντε: dual nom. pple. with the subjs., Achilles and Agamemnon

As You Read

When you read, "The anger of Achilles caused the death of many men," you don't have to stop and analyze the grammar to understand the sentence. Your goal is to be able to read Greek in the same way. In order to arrive at that point, you *do* have to ask questions about the grammar. The following are the sorts of questions to ask about the opening words of the *Iliad*.

1. Why is μῆνιν in the accusative case?

2. What is the antecedent for the relative pronoun ἥ, and of what verbs in its relative clause is ἥ the subject?

3. What tense is the verb προΐαψεν and why do you think the poet used that tense?

4. To whom does the word αὐτούς in line 4 refer?

5. What is the force of the particle δή in line 6?

Making Sense of It

The "Making Sense of It" passages are pre-readings that have been unmetrically altered to supply elided letters and occasionally to suggest implied words. In addition, variant font styles demonstrate which words are working together. Use the notes provided on the opposite page, as well as the vocabulary aids both there and in the back of the book (pp. 116–22). You may want to make your own list of vocabulary words and grammatical questions.

Summary

The *Iliad* is not simply a war story; it is a story about the cost of anger. In the opening lines, the poet asks the Muse of poetry to sing the story of Achilles and his destructive rage.

> **μῆνιν** ἄειδε, θεά, Πηληϊάδεω Ἀχιλῆος
>
> **οὐλομένην,** ἣ μυρί(α) Ἀχαιοῖς ἄλγε(α) ἔθηκε,
>
> **πολλὰς** δ(ὲ) **ἰφθίμους ψυχὰς** Ἄϊδι προΐαψεν
>
> ἡρώων, αὐτοὺς δὲ ἑλώρια τεῦχε κύνεσσιν
>
> 5   οἰωνοῖσί τε πᾶσι, Διὸς δ(ὲ) ἐτελείετο βουλή,
>
> ἐξ οὗ δὴ τὰ πρῶτα διαστήτην ἐρίσαντε
>
> Ἀτρεΐδης τε ἄναξ ἀνδρῶν καὶ δῖος Ἀχιλλεύς.

WHAT HOMER ACTUALLY COMPOSED

Vocabulary

ἀείδω, ἀείσομαι, ἄεισα, sing

Ἄϊδης, -αο, ὁ, Hades, i.e., the Underworld

ἄλγος, -εος, τό, pain, distress

Ἀτρεΐδης, -αο, ὁ, son of Atreus, i.e., Agamemnon

Ἀχαιοί, -ῶν, οἱ, Achaeans

Ἀχιλ(λ)εύς, -ῆος, ὁ, Achilles

διΐστημι, διαστήσω, διέστησα / διέστην, διέστηκα, διεστάθην, stand apart

ἔλωρ, ——, τό, spoil, prey

ἐρίζω, ——, ἔρισα, quarrel

Ζεύς, Διός, ὁ, Zeus

ἴφθιμος, -ον, strong

μῆνις, -ιος, ἡ, wrath, ire

οἰωνός, -οῦ, ὁ, bird

οὐλόμενος, -η, -ον, destroying, destructive

Πηληϊάδης, -εω, ὁ, son of Peleus

προϊάπτω, προϊάψω, προΐαψα, throw, hurl

Notes

1–7 The metrical scansion of the opening lines is laid out in the Introduction to Meter (pp. xviii–xix).

1 μῆνιν: Word position is especially important in Greek poetry. The poet positions "anger" as the poem's first word to signal his main theme. The verb ἄειδε reminds us that epic poetry was sung to an instrument similar to the guitar.

Πηληϊάδεω: a patronymic epithet, "son of . . ."; the final two vowels of this word must be pronounced as a single sound, a process called synizesis (p. xviii). Mention of Peleus brings to mind the background of the war in Troy. Tradition held that it was at the marriage of Peleus and Thetis that the trouble began, when the goddess Eris, "Strife," incited a quarrel among the goddesses by tossing out a golden apple marked, "for the most beautiful." Keep in mind that the Index of Significant Names (Appendix B, pp. 116–17) may be consulted in reference to all significant names that appear in the readings.

μῆνιν . . . Ἀχιλῆος: The poet has bracketed this first line with the words "anger," and "of Achilles," adding emphasis to his theme.

2 οὐλομένην: modifies μῆνιν in the same position of the previous line. The poet may separate related words to put them in particularly emphatic places. By placing οὐλομένην at the beginning of a new line, he draws the audience forward and speeds the movement of the narrative. This device is called EN-JAMBMENT (terms in SMALL CAPS are referenced in the Index of Figures of Speech, Appendix A, pp. 108–13) and ancient composers of verse, particularly epic poetry, used it often. Watch for it!

μυρί᾽ . . . ἄλγε᾽: Both have lost their final vowel to elision, as is regular when a word beginning with a vowel follows.

μυρί᾽ Ἀχαιοῖς ἄλγε᾽: Note that the Achaeans are bracketed by "thousands of pains." The poet literally surrounds the Greeks with suffering.

3 πολλὰς δ᾽ ἰφθίμους ψυχάς: Remember that not all words in agreement look alike: ψυχάς is modified by ἰφθίμους, just as by πολλάς. Focus on recognizing the case, number, and gender of a substantive, and then find those adjs. that have the same *grammatical* ending.

4 ἑλώρια: One might expect elision with the preceding δέ, but the conservative poetic tradition preserves the structure of an initial "w" sound, subsequently lost from the noun, producing a form of hiatus (see p. xviii).

6 τὰ πρῶτα: a substantive phrase used adverbially; neut. acc. adjs. are commonly used this way

7 Ἀτρεΐδης: four syllables

ἄναξ: Again, the tradition preserves the structure of a lost initial "w" (the Greek "digamma") preventing elision with the preceding τε; *wanax* famously appears in the Linear B records (p. xiv).

Ἀτρεΐδης . . . Ἀχιλλεύς: The poet has cleverly bracketed the line with the names of the two principal figures in the story, Agamemnon—here called Atreides, "the son of Atreus"—and Achilles. Throughout the poem this device, a form of HYPERBATON, serves to emphasize certain words or ideas. Note also the ALLITERATION within this line. Finally, contrast the spelling of Achilles' name to his name as it appears in the first line. The long tradition of the poetic language embraces multiple dialects, and allows the poet to be inconsistent in small ways that are metrically useful, and that may further "elevate" the poetic speech.

As It Was

μῆνιν ἄειδε, θεά, Πηληϊάδεω Ἀχιλῆος

οὐλομένην, ἣ μυρί' Ἀχαιοῖς ἄλγε' ἔθηκε,

πολλὰς δ' ἰφθίμους ψυχὰς Ἄϊδι προΐαψεν

ἡρώων, αὐτοὺς δὲ ἑλώρια τεῦχε κύνεσσιν

5 οἰωνοῖσί τε πᾶσι, Διὸς δ' ἐτελείετο βουλή,

ἐξ οὗ δὴ τὰ πρῶτα διαστήτην ἐρίσαντε

Ἀτρεΐδης τε ἄναξ ἀνδρῶν καὶ δῖος Ἀχιλλεύς.

AFTER READING WHAT HOMER COMPOSED

1. What characteristics of Homeric epic can you discover from the opening line of the *Iliad*?

2. The poet emphasizes anger by putting that word first in the poem. How does he reinforce the theme of anger throughout these opening lines? Why is anger such an important topic?

3. Bracketing emphasizes certain important words or ideas. Can you find two examples of this in the lines above (besides those already noted)? Why do you think the poet would choose to emphasize those places?

4. What evidence is there in the opening lines for the intervention of gods in human affairs? Do you think that such intervention will be a significant element in the poem?

5. What is the effect of referring to characters in reference to the names of their fathers?

6. If you were composing an epic today, what would you take as your theme? Why? Who would be the main characters?

READING 2

The Source of the Plague is Revealed, and the Priest Chryses Comes to Ransom His Daughter

(Iliad 1.8–21)

BEFORE YOU READ WHAT HOMER COMPOSED

Introduction

The poet has a difficult job in the opening section of the poem. He must set the stage for the action quickly, introduce the principal characters and give us some sense of who they are, and he must provide just enough background information so that we can understand what is happening without delaying the narrative.

In the first passage we learned that anger would devastate the Greeks, and we also learned who would be most involved. In these next lines we find that the quarrel is a complicated affair.

Keep This Grammar in Mind — COMPLEMENTARY AND IMPERATIVE INFINITIVES

Infinitives have many uses in Greek. Let's look at just two: complementary infinitives and infinitives used to give imperative commands. You will see both fairly often in Homer's Greek.

The **complementary infinitive** completes the meaning of another verb. For example, in the English sentence, "you ought to fight that battle," the infinitive "to fight" completes the main verb, "you ought." In this way, the complementary infinitive fills out, or "complements," the meaning of the main verb. Similarly, in the first line of the reading below, Homer asks τίς . . . ξυνέηκε μάχεσθαι, "who . . . brought them together *to fight*?"

Homer also uses infinitives to express commands. He may even use conjugated imperative forms side by side with **imperative** infinitives—with both expressing commands—as λύσαιτε and δέχεσθαι in line 20, below. Such apparent inconsistency in usage is one of the hallmarks of Homer's poetry. As you read through the selections, watch for infinitives and note their uses.

Stopping for Some Practice — COMPLEMENTARY AND IMPERATIVE INFINITIVES

The following passages come from the reading below. Locate the infinitive(s) in each sentence, and write the first principal part and the usage for each infinitive.

1. τίς . . . σφωε θεῶν ἔριδι ξυνέηκε μάχεσθαι;

   (1ˢᵗ principal part) _____ (usage) _____

2. ὑμῖν μὲν θεοὶ δοῖεν [opt. of wish < δίδωμι] . . . / ἐκπέρσαι Πριάμοιο [= Πριάμου] πόλιν, εὖ δ᾽ οἴκαδ᾽ ἱκέσθαι.

   (1ˢᵗ principal part) _____ (usage) _____

   (1ˢᵗ principal part) _____ (usage) _____

3. παῖδα δ᾽ ἐμοὶ λύσαιτε φίλην, τὰ δ᾽ ἄποινα δέχεσθαι.

   (1ˢᵗ principal part) _____ (usage) _____

Keep This Grammar in Mind — DEALING WITH DIALECT: INFINITIVES

Because of the variety of dialects in the Homeric poems, Homeric infinitives have a variety of forms. Here are all possible present active infinitives for the verb εἰμί:

εἶναι   ἔμεν   ἔμμεν   ἔμεναι   ἔμμεναι

There are similar variants for the future infinitive:

ἔσεσθαι   ἔσσεσθαι

For λύω we find the following present active infinitives:

λύειν   λῦμεν   λύμεναι   λύεμεν   λυέμεναι

There are similar variants for the future and aorist infinitives (e.g., λυσέμεν, λυσέμεναι; λυσάμεν, λυσάμεναι).

As you know, only one active infinitive form for each conjugation is found in Attic prose (e.g., εἶναι, λύειν). The number of Homeric infinitive forms may seem great in comparison, but is in fact limited. Once you have mastered these endings (in particular -μεν and -μεναι), you will find that they apply to all verbs.

There is no difference in meaning among the various forms; they are used for metrical convenience, and reflect the spread of the various Greek dialects that contributed to the development of Homeric poetry. Be sure to watch for these infinitives and keep a list of those you find troublesome.

Helping You Read What Homer Composed

Vocabulary

ἅζομαι, please, gratify

ἀπερείσιος, -ον, boundless

ἄποινα, -ων, τά, ransom

Ἀπόλλων, -ωνος, ὁ, Apollo

ἀρητήρ, -ῆρος, ὁ, priest

ἀτιμάζω, —, ἠτίμασα, dishonor

Ἀτρεΐδης, -αο, ὁ, son of Atreus, i.e., Agamemnon

Ἀχαιοί, -ῶν, οἱ, Achaeans

ἑκηβόλος, -ον, far darter, far shooter, *epithet of Apollo*

ἐκπέρθω, ἐκπέρσω, ἐξέπερσα, destroy thoroughly; sack

ἔρις, -ιδος, ἡ, strife

ἐϋκνήμις, -ιδος, well-greaved, *epithet of Achaeans*

Ζεύς, Διός, ὁ, Zeus

θυγάτηρ, -τρός, ἡ, daughter

κοσμήτωρ, -ορος, ὁ, leader

Λητώ, Λητοῦς, ἡ, Leto

λίσσομαι, —, ἐλ(λ)ισάμην, beg

νοῦσος, -ου, ἡ, disease, sickness

ξυνίημι / συνίημι, ξυνήσω, ξυνέηκα, —, —, ξυνείθην, send together

ὀλέκω, destroy, kill; *in pass.*, die

οὕνεκα, < οὗ + ἕνεκα, "because of which (fact)"

Πρίαμος, -οιο, ὁ, Priam

σκῆπτρον, -ου, τό, scepter

στέμμα, -ατος, τό, wreath, ribbon

στρατός, -οῦ, ὁ, army

σφωε, *dual pron.*, the two

χολόω, χολώσω, ἐχόλωσα, —, κεχόλωμαι, ἐχολώθην, enrage; *in mid. / pass.*, be angry

χρύσεος, -η, -ον, golden

Χρύσης, -ου, ὁ, Chryses

Notes

8   τίς ... θεῶν: partit. gen., "who among the gods ... "

σφωε: acc. dual of the personal pron. σφεῖς, "those two"

9   Λητοῦς καὶ Διὸς υἱός: i.e., Apollo

Λητοῦς: gen., contraction of Λητῶος

ὁ: Homer often uses the definite article as a pron.

βασιλῆϊ: dat. of interest, "(raging) at the king"

χολωθείς: aor. pass. pple.

10   νοῦσον: rare 2nd declen. fem.; Attic = νόσον

ὦρσε: aor. < ὄρνυμι

ὀλέκοντο: impf. pass., "were dying"; again, note the lack of augment

11   ἀρητῆρα: in apposition with the priest's name, Χρύσην

12   νῆας: acc. pl. < νηῦς (Attic = ναῦς)

13   λυσόμενος: fut. pples. regularly show motivation, "intending to free ... "

16   Ἀτρεΐδα ... δύω ... κοσμήτορε: all dual in form, referring to the two sons of Atreus, Menelaus and Agamemnon

19   δοῖεν: aor. opt. of wish < δίδωμι

ἐκπέρσαι ... ἱκέσθαι: aor. infins. dependent on δοῖεν

Πριάμοιο: Attic = Πριάμου; watch for the frequent Homeric 2nd declension gen. sing., -οιο

20   ἁζόμενοι: referring to the Achaeans, the subjs. of the aor. imperat. λύσαιτε and the infin. δέχεσθαι, used here as an imperat.

As You Read

1. Who is the subject of ὦρσε in line 10?

2. Who is the subject of ἠτίμασεν in line 11?

3. Who is speaking in lines 17–21?

4. In what case are the nouns in line 17?

Summary

Homer relates the source of the dispute between Agamemnon and Achilles. Agamemnon had captured a city allied with the Trojans and seized the daughter of a priest of Apollo. The priest, Chryses, offers to ransom his daughter, but Agamemnon refuses and sends him away, whereupon the priest calls down a plague upon the Greeks.

Making Sense of It

τίς τ(ε) ἄρ σφωε θεῶν ἔριδι ξυνέηκε μάχεσθαι;

Λητοῦς καὶ Διὸς υἱός [sc. Ἀπόλλων]· ὁ γὰρ βασιλῆϊ χολωθεὶς

10   **νοῦσον** ἀνὰ στρατὸν ὦρσε **κακήν,** ὀλέκοντο δὲ λαοί,

οὕνεκα τὸν Χρύσην ἠτίμασεν ἀρητῆρα

Ἀτρεΐδης· ὁ [sc. Χρύσης] γὰρ ἦλθε θοὰς ἐπὶ νῆας Ἀχαιῶν

λυσόμενός τε θύγατρα φέρων τ(ε) ἀπερείσι(α) ἄποινα

στέμματ(α) ἔχων ἐν χερσὶν **ἑκηβόλου Ἀπόλλωνος**

15   χρυσέῳ ἀνὰ σκήπτρῳ, καὶ λίσσετο πάντας Ἀχαιούς,

Ἀτρεΐδα δὲ μάλιστα **δύω, κοσμήτορε** λαῶν·

"Ἀτρεΐδαι τε καὶ ἄλλοι ἐϋκνήμιδες Ἀχαιοί,

ὑμῖν μὲν **θεοὶ** δοῖεν Ὀλύμπια δώματ(α) **ἔχοντες**

ἐκπέρσαι Πριάμοιο πόλιν, εὖ δ(ὲ) οἴκαδ(ε) ἱκέσθαι·

20   παῖδα δ(ὲ) ἐμοὶ λύσαιτε φίλην, τὰ δ(ὲ) ἄποινα δέχεσθαι,

(ὑμεῖς) ἁζόμενοι Διὸς υἱὸν ἑκηβόλον Ἀπόλλωνα."

WHAT HOMER ACTUALLY COMPOSED

Vocabulary

ἅζομαι, please, gratify

ἀπερείσιος, -ον, boundless

ἄποινα, -ων, τά, ransom

Ἀπόλλων, -ωνος, ὁ, Apollo

ἀρητήρ, -ῆρος, ὁ, priest

ἀτιμάζω, ——, ἠτίμασα, dishonor

Ἀτρεΐδης, -αο, ὁ, son of Atreus, i.e., Agamemnon

Ἀχαιοί, -ων, οἱ, Achaeans

ἑκηβόλος, -ον, far darter, far shooter, *epithet of Apollo*

ἐκπέρθω, ἐκπέρσω, ἐξέπερσα, destroy thoroughly; sack

ἔρις, -ιδος, ἡ, strife

ἐϋκνήμις, -ιδος, well-greaved, *epithet of Achaeans*

Ζεύς, Διός, ὁ, Zeus

θυγάτηρ, -τρός, ἡ, daughter

κοσμήτωρ, -ορος, ὁ, leader

Λητώ, Λητοῦς, ἡ, Leto

λίσσομαι, ——, ἐλ(λ)ισάμην, beg

νοῦσος, -ου, ἡ, disease, sickness

ξυνίημι / συνίημι, ξυνήσω, ξυνέηκα, ——, ——, ξυνείθην, send together

ὀλέκω, destroy, kill; *in pass.*, die

οὕνεκα, < οὗ + ἕνεκα, "because of which (fact)"

Πρίαμος, -οιο, ὁ, Priam

σκῆπτρον, -ου, τό, scepter

στέμμα, -ατος, τό, wreath, ribbon

στρατός, -οῦ, ὁ, army

σφωε, *dual pron.*, the two

χολόω, χολώσω, ἐχόλωσα, ——, κεχόλωμαι, ἐχολώθην, enrage; *in mid. / pass.*, be angry

χρύσεος, -η, -ον, golden

Χρύσης, -ου, ὁ, Chryses

Notes

8   ξυνέηκε: The augment has remained separate from the vowel-initial stem.

9   Διὸς υἱός: Apollo is not named explicitly.

βασιλῆϊ: one of two Homeric words for "king," along with ἄναξ; Agamemnon's identity is withheld until the end of this long sentence

γάρ: epexegetical ("explanatory") γάρ, used to explain or fill out a previous statement

10   νοῦσον . . . κακήν: The poet has surrounded the army (στρατόν) with the "evil disease." Be on the lookout for this poetic device, a type of SYNCHESIS.

12   θοὰς ἐπὶ νῆας: The word order is standard for preps.; cf. χρυσέῳ ἀνὰ σκήπτρῳ, line 15

13   λυσόμενος: fut. pples. often express purpose, esp. after verbs of motion

14   στέμματ᾽: The priest of Apollo held a golden staff with ribbons as a sign of his office.

ἑκηβόλου: The final syllable scans short by epic correption (p. xviii); Apollo's name fills out an unusual line ending of heavy spondaic syllables (as also in line 21 in the same position).

15   χρυσέῳ: scans as two syllables by synizesis (p. xviii), while the final syllable scans light by epic correption.

18–20 μὲν . . . δὲ . . . δὲ . . . δέ: Carefully note these signposts, as they establish the flow of the verse.

19   Πριάμοιο: This 2nd declension gen. sing. ending, -οιο, is used in the Bronze Age Greek Linear B tablets (p. xiv).

20   παῖδα . . . φίλην: The adj. is artfully delayed (SYNCHESIS)

λύσαιτε . . . δέχεσθαι: It may seem peculiar to see both an imperative and an infinitive used as an imperative in the same line, but it is not unusual to see such variation when one form fits the requirements of the meter better than another. Nevertheless, some scholars divide λύσαιτε into λῦσαί τε, making the two infinitives parallel.

As It Was

τίς τ᾿ ἄρ σφωε θεῶν ἔριδι ξυνέηκε μάχεσθαι;

Λητοῦς καὶ Διὸς υἱός· ὁ γὰρ βασιλῆϊ χολωθεὶς

10   νοῦσον ἀνὰ στρατὸν ὦρσε κακήν, ὀλέκοντο δὲ λαοί,

οὕνεκα τὸν Χρύσην ἠτίμασεν ἀρητῆρα

Ἀτρεΐδης· ὁ γὰρ ἦλθε θοὰς ἐπὶ νῆας Ἀχαιῶν

λυσόμενός τε θύγατρα φέρων τ᾿ ἀπερείσι᾿ ἄποινα

στέμματ᾿ ἔχων ἐν χερσὶν ἑκηβόλου Ἀπόλλωνος

15   χρυσέῳ ἀνὰ σκήπτρῳ, καὶ λίσσετο πάντας Ἀχαιούς,

Ἀτρεΐδα δὲ μάλιστα δύω, κοσμήτορε λαῶν·

"Ἀτρεΐδαι τε καὶ ἄλλοι ἐϋκνήμιδες Ἀχαιοί,

ὑμῖν μὲν θεοὶ δοῖεν Ὀλύμπια δώματ᾿ ἔχοντες

ἐκπέρσαι Πριάμοιο πόλιν, εὖ δ᾿ οἴκαδ᾿ ἱκέσθαι·

20   παῖδα δ᾿ ἐμοὶ λύσαιτε φίλην, τὰ δ᾿ ἄποινα δέχεσθαι,

ἁζόμενοι Διὸς υἱὸν ἑκηβόλον Ἀπόλλωνα."

AFTER READING WHAT HOMER COMPOSED

1.   Why would the god of healing cause a plague?

2.   How does the poet keep the theme of anger vivid in this reading?

3.   The root of **ἠτίμασεν** in line 11 is **τιμή**, "honor." With this in mind, where is the focus of Apollo's concern for Chryses and his daughter? How does the god's concern compare with modern expectations of the human–divine relationship?

4.   In line 13, why has Homer used a middle participle, **λυσόμενος?**

READING 3

Achilles Insults Agamemnon

(*Iliad* 1.121–29)

BEFORE YOU READ WHAT HOMER COMPOSED

Introduction

As the argument between Achilles and Agamemnon heats up, insults are exchanged. Achilles recognizes Agamemnon's position as commander of the forces, but it is clear that he has no respect for Agamemnon in personal terms. The increasing tension between them is the focus of the next several readings. Watch how Homer demonstrates the theme of anger in the leaders' respective speeches.

Keep This Grammar in Mind — THE PARTICLE κε

Homeric Greek uses particles just as often as Attic Greek, including several that are not found in Attic. One of the most common of these is κε. This word has all of the functions of ἄν, which also occurs in the Homeric poems, but κε has wider usage than ἄν. It can appear, for instance, with future indicative verbs to indicate contingency as well as with some independent uses of the subjunctive and in purpose clauses.

In this passage, αἴ κε appears in a future-more-vivid condition, in place of Attic ἐάν:

> τριπλῇ τετραπλῇ τ᾽ ἀποτείσομεν, αἴ κέ ποθι Ζεὺς
> δῷσι . . . Τροίην . . . ἐξαλαπάξαι.

> "We will pay you back three and four times over, if ever Zeus
> should grant that we take Troy."

If you gain control of particles such as κε, your reading speed and comprehension will increase τριπλῇ τετραπλῇ τε!

Keep This Grammar in Mind — COMPOUND WORDS

Learning to read any language requires making intelligent guesses about vocabulary. We do this regularly in our native tongue, but how do we develop this skill in another language? One way to speed up the acquisition of vocabulary, particularly in Greek, is by coming to grips with compound words.

Certain prepositions carry particular connotations when joined to verbs, nouns, or adjectives. An understanding of how prepositions alter the meanings of roots can sharply reduce dictionary time and increase the pleasure of reading.

Here are a few common prepositions and their meanings in compound constructions. Definitions are taken directly from the LSJ (Liddell, Scott, Jones), *A Greek – English Lexicon*, 9th ed. rev. (Oxford, 1996).

- ἀνά: up; the idea of increase or strengthening; repetition; back, backwards.
- ἐκ / ἐξ: sense of removal, out, away, off; to express completion, utterly.
- ἐπί: the ideas of support, motion, addition, etc.
- κατά: down; in accordance with; against; back; frequently to strengthen the notion of the simple word.

There are other examples in this reading and the readings that follow. You can find the meaning of a preposition used in compounds listed after the specific case usages in the LSJ lexicon (available online by searching under the title "LSJ" at http://www.perseus.tufts.edu). Look within the entry for the heading *"in compos."* Happy hunting!

Stopping for Some Practice — COMPOUND VERBS

The following clauses occur in this reading. Note the compound verbs, and write the preposition serving as the verb prefix for each, along with the meaning it contributes.

1. ἀλλὰ τὰ μὲν πολίων ἐξεπράθομεν, τὰ δέδασται.

   Preposition(s) _____ Meaning(s) _____

2. λαοὺς δ᾽ οὐκ ἐπέοικε παλίλλογα ταῦτ᾽ ἐπαγείρειν.

   Preposition(s) _____ Meaning(s) _____

3. αὐτὰρ Ἀχαιοὶ τριπλῇ τετραπλῇ τ᾽ ἀποτείσομεν.

   Preposition(s) _____ Meaning(s) _____

4. αἴ κέ ποθι Ζεὺς δῷσι πόλιν Τροίην εὐτείχεον ἐξαλαπάξαι.

   Preposition(s) _____ Meaning(s) _____

HELPING YOU READ WHAT HOMER COMPOSED

Vocabulary

ἀμείβω, ἀμείψω, ἤμειψα, reply; exchange
ἀποτίνω, ἀποτείσω, ἀπέτισα, pay back
Ἀτρεΐδης, -αο, ὁ, son of Atreus, i.e., Agamemnon
Ἀχαιοί, -ῶν, οἱ, Achaeans
Ἀχιλλεύς, -ῆος, ὁ, Achilles
γέρας, -αος, τό, prize of honor
δατέομαι, divide
ἐκπέρθω, ἐκπέρσω, ἐξέπερσα, sack thoroughly;
    + gen., pillage from
ἐξαλαπάζω, ἐξαλαπάξω, ἐξηλάπαξα, destroy,
    sack
ἐπαγείρω, collect together
ἐπέοικα, pf., be seemly, be proper
εὐτείχεος, -ον, well-walled

Ζεύς, Διός, ὁ, Zeus
κύδιστος, -η, -ον, most praised
μεγάθυμος, -ον, great-hearted
ξυνήϊος, -ον, common; in pl., common property
οἶδα, pf., know
παλίλλογος, -ον, gathered up again
ποδάρκης, -ες, swift-footed
προΐημι, προήσω, προέηκα, ——, ——, προείθην,
    let go; surrender
τετραπλόος, -η, -ον, fourfold
τριπλόος, -η, -ον, threefold
Τροίη, -ης, ἡ, Troy
φιλοκτέανος, -ον, lover of possessions, greedy

Notes

121 τόν: = αὐτόν
122 πάντων: partit. gen.
123 τοι: here = σοι
         δώσουσι: fut. < δίδωμι
124 τί: "at all, in any respect"; here accented because of subsequent enclitic
         ἴδμεν: < οἶδα, "we do not know of . . ."
         κείμενα: pple. < κεῖμαι
125 πολίων: < πόλις
125 τὰ . . . τά: both = αὐτά in reference to ξυνήϊα, "the spoils (that) we took, . . . those have been . . ."
         δέδασται: pf. < δατέομαι
126 ἐπέοικε: pf., but translate as pres., "it is not fitting . . ."
127 πρόες: aor. imperat. < προΐημι
127–28 Ἀχαιοί: in apposition to the 1st pl. subj. of ἀποτείσομεν
128 τριπλῇ τετραπλῇ τ': dat. fem. sings. used as advs.
         αἴ κέ: Attic = ἐάν < εἰ + ἄν
129 δῷσι: aor. subjnc. < δίδωμι; the subsequent infin. expresses the thing granted
         Τροίην εὐτείχεον: compound adjs. have no distinct fem. forms

As You Read

122–23: Who is the subject of **δώσουσι?** How do the vocatives fit into this sentence?

126: On what verb is the infinitive **ἐπαγείρειν** dependent?

129: What tense is the infinitive **ἐξαλαπάξαι?** Why is this tense appropriate?

Summary

Achilles and Agamemnon have been arguing over the plague sent by Apollo as retribution for Agamemnon's mistreatment of the priest, Chryses. In the following readings, the argument escalates as anger heats up on both sides. Agamemnon seems willing to return the girl Chryseis to her father Chryses, but he wants some material goods as compensation, so that his honor remains intact. Achilles, insulting Agamemnon in harsh terms, explains that nothing is available, but counters that the Achaeans will reward Agamemnon if they sack Troy.

Making Sense of It

τὸν δ(ὲ) ἠμείβετ(ο) ἔπειτα **ποδάρκης δῖος Ἀχιλλεύς·**

"Ἀτρεΐδη κύδιστε, φιλοκτεανώτατε πάντων,

πῶς γάρ τοι δώσουσι γέρας **μεγάθυμοι Ἀχαιοί;**

οὐδέ τί που ἴδμεν ξυνήϊα κείμενα πολλά·

125   ἀλλὰ τὰ μὲν πολίων ἐξεπράθομεν, τὰ δέδασται,

λαοὺς δ(ὲ) οὐκ ἐπέοικε παλίλλογα ταῦτ(α) ἐπαγείρειν.

ἀλλὰ σὺ μὲν νῦν τήνδε (κούρην) θεῷ πρόες· αὐτὰρ Ἀχαιοὶ

τριπλῇ τετραπλῇ τ(ε) ἀποτείσομεν, αἴ κέ ποθι Ζεὺς

δῷσι (ἡμῖν) **πόλιν Τροίην εὐτείχεον ἐξαλαπάξαι."**

WHAT HOMER ACTUALLY COMPOSED

Vocabulary

ἀμείβω, ἀμείψω, ἤμειψα, reply; exchange

ἀποτίνω, ἀποτείσω, ἀπέτισα, pay back

Ἀτρεΐδης, -αο, ὁ, son of Atreus, i.e., Agamemnon

Ἀχαιοί, -ῶν, οἱ, Achaeans

Ἀχιλλεύς, -ῆος, ὁ, Achilles

γέρας, -αος, τό, prize of honor

δατέομαι, divide

ἐκπέρθω, ἐκπέρσω, ἐξέπερσα, sack thoroughly; + gen., pillage from

ἐξαλαπάζω, ἐξαλαπάξω, ἐξηλάπαξα, destroy, sack

ἐπαγείρω, collect together

ἐπέοικα, pf., be seemly, be proper

εὐτείχεος, -ον, well-walled

Ζεύς, Διός, ὁ, Zeus

κύδιστος, -η, -ον, most praised

μεγάθυμος, -ον, great-hearted

ξυνήϊος, -ον, common; in pl., common property

οἶδα, pf., know

παλίλλογος, -ον, gathered up again

ποδάρκης, -ες, swift-footed

προΐημι, προήσω, προέηκα, —, —, προείθην, let go; surrender

τετραπλόος, -η, -ον, fourfold

τριπλόος, -η, -ον, threefold

Τροίη, -ης, ἡ, Troy

φιλοκτέανος, -ον, lover of possessions, greedy

Notes

121 τὸν δ᾽ ἠμείβετ᾽ ἔπειτα: This formulaic opening regularly introduces a response in dialogue. The remainder of the line is then filled by the name + epithet of the individual responding. Note the ASSO-NANCE of the formula.

122 Ἀτρεΐδη . . . πάντων: It is not unusual for a naming formula to occupy an entire line, here in an impressive four words.

122–29 It is easy to imagine Achilles sneering as he delivers these lines, particularly the opening couplet. He chooses words that establish his position as a champion of justice who expects his commander to work and sacrifice together with the troops. He does acknowledge Agamemnon's position (line 128) but first insists that there are unwritten rules by which the camp must operate if all are to be treated fairly (lines 123, 125–26).

124 οὐδέ τί: Scholars disagree whether these words should be read as printed, or as the more easily understood οὐ δ᾽ ἔτι, "no longer." The manuscripts preserve both readings, but most scholars adopt the reading chosen here, on the principle of "lectio difficilior," i.e., the *harder reading* is probably the correct one, since the easier reading is more likely to have been generated by a scribe who failed to grasp the original phrase.

126 παλίλλογα: a compound of πάλιν, "back," and a form of λέγω, which becomes a verb of speaking, but is rooted in the meaning "gather," much as English "recollect" means "speak (gathering from memory)."

As It Was

τὸν δ᾽ ἠμείβετ᾽ ἔπειτα ποδάρκης δῖος Ἀχιλλεύς·

"Ἀτρεΐδη κύδιστε, φιλοκτεανώτατε πάντων,

πῶς γάρ τοι δώσουσι γέρας μεγάθυμοι Ἀχαιοί;

οὐδέ τί που ἴδμεν ξυνήϊα κείμενα πολλά·

125   ἀλλὰ τὰ μὲν πολίων ἐξεπράθομεν, τὰ δέδασται,

λαοὺς δ᾽ οὐκ ἐπέοικε παλίλλογα ταῦτ᾽ ἐπαγείρειν.

ἀλλὰ σὺ μὲν νῦν τήνδε θεῷ πρόες· αὐτὰρ Ἀχαιοὶ

τριπλῇ τετραπλῇ τ᾽ ἀποτείσομεν, αἴ κέ ποθι Ζεὺς

δῶσι πόλιν Τροίην εὐτείχεον ἐξαλαπάξαι."

AFTER READING WHAT HOMER COMPOSED

1. Do you think that Achilles' response to Agamemnon's refusal is fair? Extreme? Too mild? How do you respond when you have been dealt what you perceive as an injustice?

2. What specific words or phrases indicate that the level of anger is rising for both Achilles and Agamemnon? As you read this passage aloud, notice the sound values of the words and how the various poetic sound devices contribute to the angry tone of the speakers.

3. Why do you think Achilles tells Agamemnon to release the girl to the god, rather than to her father?

4. Why has Achilles introduced Zeus into his argument against Agamemnon? How do Achilles' words to Agamemnon reflect two opposing ideas about destiny?

READING 4

Achilles and Agamemnon Intensify Their Dispute

(*Iliad* 1.130–39)

BEFORE YOU READ WHAT HOMER COMPOSED

Introduction

This passage carries on the exchange begun in Reading 3. Agamemnon recognizes Achilles' qualities (calling him "godlike" in line 131), but is in no mood to bargain with his subordinate. Agamemnon will not be deprived of his prize of honor while Achilles and the other Greeks keep theirs.

Keep This Grammar in Mind — CONDITIONS

Uncertainty is a fact of life. Consequently, people construct expressions to reflect the dependency of one action on another. Both English and ancient Greek logically set such conditional statements in balance: "If it should rain soon, then the crops would grow." Conditional sentences can also be mixed as to tense and mood: "If he had turned before, then he would be here now."

The reading in this chapter presents an example of a complex future condition. The difficult syntax reflects Homer's ability to reproduce the natural rhythm of Agamemnon's enraged threats.

> εἰ μὲν δώσουσι γέρας ... ὅπως ἀντάξιον ἔσται· εἰ δέ κε μὴ δώωσιν, ἐγὼ δέ κεν αὐτὸς ἕλωμαι ... τεὸν ... γέρας, ἢ Ὀδυσῆος ἄξω.

> "If they will grant a prize, so that it will be of equal value to what I've lost [so be it]. But if they won't, I would take your prize myself, or I will lead away the prize of Odysseus."

Stopping for Some Practice — CONDITIONS

Study these conditional sentences that you will encounter in later readings. Carefully note the tenses and moods of the verbs.

1. φεῦγε μάλ᾽, εἴ τοι θυμὸς ἐπέσσυται . . .
   [Reading 6 notes line 175, p. 34]

2. καί νύ κεν ἔνθ᾽ ἀπόλοιτο ἄναξ ἀνδρῶν Αἰνείας,
   εἰ μὴ ἄρ᾽ ὀξὺ νόησε Λιὸς θυγάτηρ . . .
   [Reading 8 notes line 311, p. 48]

3. εἰ δὲ σύ γ᾽ ἐς πόλεμον πωλήσεαι, ἦ τέ σ᾽ ὀΐω
   ῥιγήσειν . . .
   [Reading 9 notes lines 350–51, p. 58]

4. τοιοῦτοι δ᾽ εἴ πέρ μοι ἐείκοσιν ἀντεβόλησαν,
   πάντες κ᾽ αὐτόθ᾽ ὄλοντο . . .
   [Reading 13 notes lines 847–48, p. 94]

Helping You Read What Homer Composed

Vocabulary

Ἀγαμέμνων, -ονος, ὁ, Agamemnon

Αἴας, -αντος, ὁ, Ajax

ἀπαμείβω, -αμείψω, -ήμειψα, *in mid.,* answer, reply

Ἀχαιοί, -ῶν, οἱ, Achaeans

Ἀχιλ(λ)εύς, -ῆος, ὁ, Achilles

δεύω / δεύομαι, δευήσομαι, ἐδεύησα, lack, want

θεοείκελος, -η, -ον, like a god, godlike

κέλομαι, κελήσομαι, command, bid

κλέπτω, ——, ἔκλεψα, deceive; steal

κρείων, -οντος, ὁ, ruler, *esp. as epithet of Agamemnon*

Ὀδυσσεύς, -ῆος, ὁ, Odysseus

παρέρχομαι, -ελεύσομαι, -ῆλθον, pass by; outwit

περ, *intensive particle,* indeed; *concessive particle,* although

Notes

130 **τόν:** = αὐτόν, i.e., Achilles

131 **ἐών:** pple. < εἰμί, best translated as a conjugated verb with concessive force (as suggested by περ), "although you are . . . "

132 **νόῳ:** dat. of place where, "Don't be deceptive in (your) mind"

    παρελεύσεαι: 2nd sing. fut. mid. = -εσαι; here, the sigma drops out, becoming -εαι, but the vowels do not contract, unlike Attic -η

    πείσεις: fut. < πείθω

133 **ὄφρ':** Homer uses ὄφρα + subjnc. both with and without ἄν, "that you yourself hold your prize."

    αὐτός: in the nom., αὐτός, -ή, -ό is always intensive in agreement with the subj.; cf. line 137

    ἐμέ: subj. for the infin. ἧσθαι, "do you want me to sit (here) deprived . . . "

134 **κέλεαι:** pres. For the contracted form, see **παρελεύσεαι** above (line 132).

    τήνδ': i.e., the priest's daughter, Cryseis

    ἀποδοῦναι: aor. infin. < ἀποδίδωμι

135 **δώσουσι:** fut. < δίδωμι

136 **ἄρσαντες:** aor. pple. < ἀραρίσκω

    ὅπως ἀντάξιον ἔσται: The difficulty is that a command, such as "let them see to it," has been omitted, "(let them see to it) that it will be of equal value."

137 **κεν:** Homeric variant for ἄν (cf. κε), here with the subjnc. in a future-more-vivid condition

    δώωσιν: Homeric verb forms are not consistent. Here, the aor. subjnc. (< δίδωμι) lengthens the stem vowel in addition to lengthening the vowel of the personal ending.

137–39 **ἕλωμαι . . . ἰών:** This verb + pple. construction occurs often in Homeric poetry, and twice here (ἄξω ἑλών), "Perhaps I'll go and take your prize or Ajax's, or I'll take and lead away (the prize) of Odysseus."

138 **ἰών:** pres. act. pple. < εἶμι

139 **κεν . . . κεχολώσεται:** κεν used with the fut. (here the uncommon fut. pf.) shows future contingency, but here almost indicates a jussive subjnc., ". . . and let him choke on it."

As You Read

1. What is the grammatical function of **τὸν** in line 130?

2. What two moods are used in line 132 and why?

Summary

Agamemnon responds to Achilles' complaints with a clear statement of superiority. He tells Achilles not to try to deceive him, and questions why Achilles should keep a prize (γέρας) while he himself must surrender his own. Finally he threatens to seize the prize of some other Greek hero, even the prize of Achilles himself.

Making Sense of It

130　　τὸν δ(ὲ) ἀπαμειβόμενος προσέφη κρείων Ἀγαμέμνων·

　　　"**μὴ** δὴ οὕτως, ἀγαθός περ ἐών, θεοείκελ(ε) Ἀχιλλεῦ,

　　　κλέπτε νόῳ, ἐπεὶ οὐ παρελεύσε(σ)αι οὐδέ με πείσεις.

　　　ἦ ἐθέλεις, ὄφρ(α) αὐτὸς ἔχῃς γέρας, αὐτὰρ **ἔμ(ε)** αὔτως

　　　ἧσθαι **δευόμενον**, κέλε(σ)αι δέ με τήνδ(ε) ἀποδοῦναι;

135　　ἀλλ(ὰ) **εἰ μὲν** δώσουσι γέρας μεγάθυμοι Ἀχαιοί,

　　　ἄρσαντες κατὰ θυμόν, ὅπως ἀντάξιον ἔσται·

　　　εἰ δέ κε μή (μοι γέρας) δώωσιν, ἐγὼ δέ κεν αὐτὸς ἕλωμαι

　　　ἢ τεὸν (γέρας) ἢ Αἴαντος ἰὼν γέρας, ἢ Ὀδυσῆος

　　　ἄξω ἑλών· ὁ δέ κεν κεχολώσεται ὅν κεν ἵκωμαι . . .

WHAT HOMER ACTUALLY COMPOSED

Vocabulary

Ἀγαμέμνων, -ονος, ὁ, Agamemnon

Αἴας, -αντος, ὁ, Ajax

ἀπαμείβω, -αμείψω, -ήμειψα, *in mid.*, answer,
 reply

Ἀχαιοί, -ῶν, οἱ, Achaeans

Ἀχιλ(λ)εύς, -ῆος, ὁ, Achilles

δεύω / δεύομαι, δευήσομαι, ἐδεύησα, lack, want

θεοείκελος, -η, -ον, like a god, godlike

κέλομαι, κελήσομαι, command, bid

κλέπτω, ——, ἔκλεψα, deceive; steal

κρείων, -οντος, ὁ, ruler, *esp. as epithet of Agamemnon*

Ὀδυσσεύς, -ῆος, ὁ, Odysseus

παρέρχομαι, -ελεύσομαι, -ῆλθον, pass by; outwit

περ, *intensive particle,* indeed; *concessive particle,*
 although

Notes

130   τὸν δ᾽ ἀπαμειβόμενος προσέφη: another formulaic phrase for a response; the subj. of προσέφη
comprises the last part of the line

131   δή: must be pronounced together with the first syllable of the following οὕτως by synizesis

ἀγαθός περ ἐών: Both men understand their respective status, but Agamemnon's acknowledgment of
Achilles' qualities rings hollow.

132   ἐπεί: The final syllable scans short by epic correption with the following οὐ, see Introduction to Meter,
p. xviii. You can find another example of correption in the final line of this reading.

135–38   There are two conditions in these lines. The first is cast as a simple fut. with the verbs δώσουσι and
ἔσται. The second condition, however, does not fit any of the prescribed categories. Homer gives us
two subjncs. modified by the particle κε, and a fut.: δώωσιν ... ἕλωμαι ... ἄξω. While it is just possible that ἄξω may be an aor. subjnc., the indic. adds strength to Agamemnon's assertion. This may be
a bit confounding, but in fact it is just what we would expect from someone who is angry and becom-
ing irrational. Agamemnon's syntax reflects his agitated state of mind. He understands the possibility
of being denied, and thus uses subjncs. for the first two, but closes with an indic. as if to say, "I'll have
my way in the end." Finally he adds the dig in line 139 that the person whose prize he takes will be
angry. The insidious power of anger will spread.

As It Was

130   τὸν δ᾽ ἀπαμειβόμενος προσέφη κρείων Ἀγαμέμνων·

       "μὴ δὴ οὕτως, ἀγαθός περ ἐών, θεοείκελ᾽ Ἀχιλλεῦ,

       κλέπτε νόῳ, ἐπεὶ οὐ παρελεύσεαι οὐδέ με πείσεις.

       ἦ ἐθέλεις, ὄφρ᾽ αὐτὸς ἔχῃς γέρας, αὐτὰρ ἔμ᾽ αὔτως

       ἧσθαι δευόμενον, κέλεαι δέ με τήνδ᾽ ἀποδοῦναι;

135   ἀλλ᾽ εἰ μὲν δώσουσι γέρας μεγάθυμοι Ἀχαιοί,

       ἄρσαντες κατὰ θυμόν, ὅπως ἀντάξιον ἔσται·

       εἰ δέ κε μὴ δώωσιν, ἐγὼ δέ κεν αὐτὸς ἕλωμαι

       ἢ τεὸν ἢ Αἴαντος ἰὼν γέρας, ἢ Ὀδυσῆος

       ἄξω ἑλών· ὁ δέ κεν κεχολώσεται ὅν κεν ἵκωμαι . . . "

AFTER READING WHAT HOMER COMPOSED

1. Is Agamemnon's position fair? Is it reasonable for him to be without a prize of honor when all the other Achaeans retain their prizes? Why or why not? Remember that the sorts of gifts one received reflected one's position in society.

2. What are we to make of Agamemnon's choice of words in this passage? Look back at Achilles' reply in the previous reading. How does he address Agamemnon at the opening of that reply? What is Agamemnon's parallel phrase here, and how are we to reconcile that with what follows? Do you think Agamemnon is sincere when he refers to Achilles as ἀγαθός?

READING 5

Achilles Harshly Insults Agamemnon

(*Iliad* 1.148–60)

BEFORE YOU READ WHAT HOMER COMPOSED

Introduction

As the argument between Achilles and Agamemnon becomes increasingly hot, the insults continue on both sides. Achilles is determined to demonstrate that Agamemnon is unsuited to be the commander-in-chief, and in doing so he insults Agamemnon's honor. This becomes a source of deeper anger between the two men.

Keep This Grammar in Mind — GENITIVE CASE

Although you may be accustomed to thinking of the genitive case primarily as showing possession, it is also commonly used to show source. If one thinks of it this way, unusual uses seem quite regular. The following list, although not complete, provides a sample of the varied uses of the genitive:

- The first and last words of the opening line of the *Iliad* work together to make a **subjective genitive:** μῆνιν . . . Ἀχιλῆος, "the wrath . . . of Achilles."

- The genitive is also used with prepositions denoting movement away from a source (e.g., ἀπό, ἐξ).

Recall these other uses of the genitive:

- A genitive object follows many types of verbs: verbs of filling, touching, forgetting, remembering, ruling, and others.

- Genitives appear in the context of comparatives to express the second noun in the comparison.

- The genitive is used to express the **time within which** an action occurs.

- Do not forget the **genitive absolute,** which can bury a full clause in just a genitive noun and circumstantial participle.

- The genitive often works like an adjective; it describes or limits another noun. Thus you might also think of it as the descriptive or adjectival case.

Watch for different uses of the genitive in the reading below.

Dealing with Dialect — Genitive Case

The genitive case in Homeric Greek shows a wide variety of possible endings. These include uncontracted forms preserving two vowels that in Attic Greek would combine into a single sound.

Here is a list of the most common genitive endings in the 1ˢᵗ and 2ⁿᵈ declensions:

1ˢᵗ declension:	singular:	-ας,	-ης,	-αο,	-εω
	plural:	-ῶν,	-άων,	-έων	
2ⁿᵈ declension	singular:	-οιο,	-οο,	-ου,	
	plural:	-ων			

Most 3ʳᵈ-declension nouns are as in Attic Greek, but some show uncontracted forms, e.g., ἔπος, ἔπεος:

3ʳᵈ declension	singular:	-ος
	plural:	-ων

Some pronouns also have peculiar genitive singular forms:

ἐγώ:	ἐμεῖο,	ἐμεῦ,	ἐμέθεν
σύ:	σεῖο,	σεῦ,	σέθεν

Familiarity with these endings will save time otherwise spent in the grammars and lexica.

Stopping for Some Practice — Genitives

The following appear in this and the next reading. Referring to the grammar reviews above, identify and note the use of each genitive.

1. πῶς **τίς** τοι πρόφρων ἔπεσιν πείθηται Ἀχαιῶν;

    Use _____

2. οὐ γὰρ ἐγὼ **Τρώων ἕνεκ᾽** ἤλυθον αἰχμητάων / δεῦρο μαχησόμενος.

    Use _____

3. **σέθεν** δ᾽ ἐγὼ οὐκ **ἀλεγίζω**, / οὐδ᾽ **ὄθομαι κοτέοντος**·

    Uses _____

4. τὸν δ᾽ ἠμείβετο ἔπειτα **ἄναξ ἀνδρῶν** Ἀγαμέμνων·

    Use _____

5. **φέρτερός** εἰμι **σέθεν**.

    Use _____

HELPING YOU READ WHAT HOMER COMPOSED

Vocabulary

αἰχμητής, -οῦ, ὁ, spearman

ἀναιδείη, -ης, ἡ, shamelessness

Ἀχαιοί, -ῶν, οἱ, Achaeans

Ἀχιλ(λ)εύς, -ῆος, ὁ, Achilles

βωτιάνειρα, man-feeding, *epithet of fertile earth*

δηλέομαι, δηλήσομαι, ἐδηλησάμην, do harm

ἐπιέννυμι, ἐπιέσ(σ)ω, ἐπιέσσα, ——, ἐπιεῖμαι, be clothed in

ἕπομαι, ἕψομαι, ἑσπόμην, follow

ἔρχομαι, ἐλεύσομαι, ἦλθον, ἐλήλυθα, go, come

Μενέλαος, -ου, ὁ, Menelaus

μετατρέπομαι, care for, be concerned about

Τρῶοι, -ων, οἱ, Trojans

ὑπόδρα, darkly, with a scowl

Φθίη, -ης, ἡ, Phthia

Notes

148 πόδας: < πούς

πόδας ὠκὺς Ἀχιλλεύς: Achilles' most famous epithet, "swift-footed"; lit., "swift (in respect to his) feet"

149 ἀναιδείην ἐπιειμένε: acc. of respect with a voc. pf. mid. pple., "clothed in shamelessness"

150 τίς: indefinite, with accent from subsequent enclitic

πείθηται: subjnc., here used in a deliberative question; the two infins. that follow are dependent on πείθηται.

151 ἀνδράσιν: dat. after μάχεσθαι, "to fight against men"

152 ἤλυθον: aor. < ἔρχομαι

153 μαχησόμενος: fut. pples. can express purpose, esp. following a verb of motion (here, ἤλυθον)

τί: indefinite, with accent from subsequent enclitic

154 ἤλασαν: aor. < ἐλαύνω

157 οὔρεα: Attic = ὄρη < ὄρος

158 ἀναιδές, voc., compound of the negative prefix ἀ(ν)- and αἰδώς, "lacking shame"

σοὶ . . . ἅμ': The dat. is dependent on ἑσπόμεθ'; ἅμα is an independent adv. here.

ὄφρα σὺ χαίρης: purpose clause

159 κυνῶπα: voc., compound of κυών, "dog," and ὦπα, "eye, face"

160 τῶν: = αὐτῶν; definite articles. can be used as prons. in Homer, "these things"

As You Read

1. Watch for the word **τιμή** in the text. When does Achilles introduce the idea and what effect does it have?

2. Animal imagery will also appear in future readings. In this instance, but for the gravity of his anger, Achilles' EPITHET for Agamemnon, **κυνῶπα**, would seem almost comical. But consider Achilles' statement following this taunt. Then review the poet's reference to dogs in Reading 1. What darker implication does it bring to the accusation Achilles levels at Agamemnon here?

Summary

Achilles, amid even more insults, carries on the argument with Agamemnon, and points out that he himself has no direct quarrel with the Trojans. Rather he puts the blame for the war squarely on the shoulders of the sons of Atreus. Achilles' rhetoric becomes much sharper here, both in general terms and in specifics such as word choice.

Making Sense of It

τὸν δ(ὲ) ἄρ(α) ὑπόδρα ἰδὼν προσέφη πόδας ὠκὺς Ἀχιλλεύς·

"ὤ μοι, ἀναιδείην ἐπιειμένε, κερδαλεόφρον,

150   πῶς τίς τοι **πρόφρων** ἔπεσιν πείθηται Ἀχαιῶν

ἢ ὁδὸν ἐλθέμεναι ἢ ἀνδράσιν ἶφι μάχεσθαι;

οὐ γὰρ ἐγὼ Τρώων ἕνεκ(α) ἤλυθον αἰχμητάων

δεῦρο **μαχησόμενος**, ἐπεὶ οὔ τί μοι αἴτιοί εἰσιν·

οὐ γὰρ πώ ποτ(ε) ἐμὰς βοῦς ἤλασαν οὐδὲ μὲν ἵππους,

155   οὐδέ ποτ(ε) ἐν **Φθίῃ ἐριβώλακι βωτιανείρῃ**

καρπὸν ἐδηλήσαντ(ο), ἐπεὶ ἦ μάλα πολλὰ μεταξὺ

οὔρεά τε σκιόεντα θάλασσά τε ἠχήεσσα·

ἀλλὰ σοί, ὦ μέγ(α) ἀναιδές, ἅμ(α) ἑσπόμεθ(α), ὄφρα σὺ χαίρῃς,

τιμὴν ἀρνύμενοι Μενελάῳ σοί τε, κυνῶπα,

160   πρὸς Τρώων· τῶν οὔ τι μετατρέπῃ οὐδ(ὲ) ἀλεγίζεις·

WHAT HOMER ACTUALLY COMPOSED

Vocabulary

αἰχμητής, -οῦ, ὁ, spearman

ἀναιδείη, -ης, ἡ, shamelessness

Ἀχαιοί, -ῶν, οἱ, Achaeans

Ἀχιλ(λ)εύς, -ῆος, ὁ, Achilles

βωτιάνειρα, man-feeding, *epithet of fertile earth*

δηλέομαι, δηλήσομαι, ἐδηλησάμην, do harm

ἐπιέννυμι, ἐπιέσ(σ)ω, ἐπιέσσα, —, ἐπιεῖμαι, be clothed in

ἕπομαι, ἕψομαι, ἑσπόμην, follow

ἔρχομαι, ἐλεύσομαι, ἦλθον, ἐλήλυθα, go, come

Μενέλαος, -ου, ὁ, Menelaus

μετατρέπομαι, care for, be concerned about

Τρῶοι, -ων, οἱ, Trojans

ὑπόδρα, darkly, with a scowl

Φθίη, -ης, ἡ, Phthia

Notes

148   ὑπόδρα ἰδών: Homer shows us Achilles changed. This brief phrase demonstrates well the economy with which Homer works. Two words suffice to indicate that Achilles is now at a very different level of anger, and they foreshadow the invective that follows. We are well set up for the flurry of insults.

149   Another full line devoted to naming—and insulting—Agamemnon (cf. line 122 in Reading 3, p. 18).

It is difficult to imagine words that would cut Agamemnon more deeply than being called a shameless coward in front of his assembled troops. See also line 158.

μοι: The syllable is shortened by correption (p. xviii). Can you find other instances of epic correption in this reading?

150–60   Observe Homer's careful use of particular consonants and vowels. Hear the lines and gauge the effect of the ALLITERATION of specific consonants (s, p, t, k, etc.).

152–53   The first line ends with heavy spondees, but is followed by a run of dactyls. What effect does this arrangement have on the narrative? Can you find the other pair of lines in this reading characterized by a spondaic line followed by dactyls?

153   μαχησόμενος: There is no obvious explanation why the final syllable scans long, but the strong sense pause after the word helps smooth the irregularity.

As It Was

τὸν δ᾽ ἄρ᾽ ὑπόδρα ἰδὼν προσέφη πόδας ὠκὺς Ἀχιλλεύς·

"ὤ μοι, ἀναιδείην ἐπιειμένε, κερδαλεόφρον,

150   πῶς τίς τοι πρόφρων ἔπεσιν πείθηται Ἀχαιῶν

ἢ ὁδὸν ἐλθέμεναι ἢ ἀνδράσιν ἶφι μάχεσθαι;

οὐ γὰρ ἐγὼ Τρώων ἕνεκ᾽ ἤλυθον αἰχμητάων

δεῦρο μαχησόμενος, ἐπεὶ οὔ τί μοι αἴτιοί εἰσιν·

οὐ γάρ πώ ποτ᾽ ἐμὰς βοῦς ἤλασαν οὐδὲ μὲν ἵππους,

155   οὐδέ ποτ᾽ ἐν Φθίῃ ἐριβώλακι βωτιανείρῃ

καρπὸν ἐδηλήσαντ᾽, ἐπεὶ ἦ μάλα πολλὰ μεταξὺ

οὔρεά τε σκιόεντα θάλασσά τε ἠχήεσσα·

ἀλλὰ σοί ὦ μέγ᾽ ἀναιδές, ἅμ᾽ ἑσπόμεθ᾽, ὄφρα σὺ χαίρῃς,

τιμὴν ἀρνύμενοι Μενελάῳ σοί τε, κυνῶπα,

160   πρὸς Τρώων· τῶν οὔ τι μετατρέπῃ οὐδ᾽ ἀλεγίζεις·

AFTER READING WHAT HOMER COMPOSED

1. Discuss Achilles' arguments in 1.152–57. Do you think he is justified in adopting this line of argument? Why or why not? What has Achilles done in general terms by arguing as he does, and what is the effect of his words?

2. Homer is clearly manipulating his audience through his mastery over words. Discuss the power of the subtle devices that force us to pay closer attention to a particular line or thought. How and why do specific sounds have such an effect on us? Can you find any contemporary writing, perhaps a newspaper editorial or a speech by a major political figure, that employs similar devices?

READING 6

Agamemnon Vows to Take Achilles' Spear-bride

(*Iliad* 1.172–87)

BEFORE YOU READ WHAT HOMER COMPOSED

Introduction

In this final selection from Book 1, Agamemnon effectively seals the fate of Achilles. The excerpt concludes with Agamemnon promising to prove his strength by taking for himself Briseis, the girl Achilles loves and a symbol of his honor. Following this exchange, Achilles is prevented from killing Agamemnon only by the intervention of Athena.

Keep This Grammar in Mind — DATIVE CASE

The dative case is called in Greek πτῶσις δωτική, the "case of giving." You may have heard it called the "2/4" case because it is often translated with the prepositions "to" and "for," but the dative, like the genitive (see p. 26), has multiple uses.

- The dative is most closely associated with the **indirect object,** often in the context of a verb concerned with giving, including giving commands.

- The **dative of the possessor** expresses ownership by putting the possessor into the dative case while the direct object takes the owner's place as the subject. The statement, "Agamemnon has friends," would become, "Friends there are for Agamemnon." It sounds like Yoda Greek!

- The **dative of interest** represents the person who stands to gain or lose the most when a particular action is performed.

- The dative is also used with prepositions (e.g., ἐν, ὑπό), generally when no motion is shown (but see p. 39, below).

- The dative is used to express the **time at which** an action occurs.

- The dative is used with many adjectives, including those concerned with friendship, hostility, and equality.

- The dative is also used as the object of compound verbs and of many verbs whose meaning implies hostility or friendliness.

Dealing with Dialect — Dative Case

Review the following endings for the dative case. On a separate sheet of paper decline at least one noun in the reading below from each of the three declension patterns.

1st declension
Singular: -η   -α
Plural: -ῃσι   -ῃς   -αις

2nd declension
Singular: -ῳ
Plural: -οισι, -οις

3rd declension:
Singular: -ι
Plural: -εσσι, -εσι,   -σι,   -ουσι, -ξι, -ψι, -οσι, -ασι, -ευσι, -ωσι, -ισι

The 3rd declension plural has a broad range of possibilities. Observe, however, that most are reducible to the ending **-σι** preceded by a stem consonant, vowel, or diphthong. When considering a stem that ends with a consonant, remember:

γ   κ   χ   +   σι   =   ξι

β   π   φ   +   σι   =   ψι

δ   τ   θ   +   σι   =   σι

Stopping for Some Practice — Datives

The following appear in this reading. Referring to the grammar review above, identify and note the use of each dative.

1. εἰ μάλα καρτερός ἐσσι, θεός που σοὶ τό γε ἔδωκεν.

    Use _____

2. οἴκαδ᾽ ἰὼν σὺν νηυσί τε σῆς καὶ σοῖς ἑτάροισι / Μυρμιδόνεσσιν ἄνασσε.

    Uses _____   _____

3. ἀπειλήσω δὲ τοι ὧδε· τὴν μὲν ἐγὼ σὺν νηΐ πέμψω . . .

    Uses _____   _____

4. . . . ὄφρα στυγέῃ δὲ καὶ ἄλλος ἶσον ἐμοὶ φάσθαι.

    Use _____

HELPING YOU READ WHAT HOMER COMPOSED

Vocabulary

ἀλεγίζω, have regard for, + *gen.*

ἄντην, face to face, openly against

ἀπειλέω, ἀπειλήσω, ἠπείλησα, declare; promise

Ἀπόλλων, -ωνος, ὁ, Apollo

ἀφαιρέω, ἀφαιρήσω, ἀφεῖλον, take away

Βρισηΐς, -ΐδος, ἡ, Briseis

γέρας, -αος, τό, prize of honor

διοτρεφής, -ές, cherished by Zeus

ἐπισσεύω, ——, ἐπέσ(σ)ευα, ——, ἐπέσ(σ)υμαι, ἐπεσ(σ)ύθην, set upon; *in pass.*, be eager, be incited

ἔρις, -ιδος, ἡ, strife

ἐχθρός, -ή, -όν, hateful to, + *dat.*

Ζεὺς, Διός, ὁ, Zeus

ἴσος, -η, -ον, equal to, + *dat.*

καλλιπάρῃος, -ον, fair-cheeked

καρτερός, -ά, -όν, physically strong, powerful

κοτέω, ——, ἐκότεσ(σ)α, κεκότη(κ)α, resent, be angry at

λίσσομαι, ——, ἐλ(λ)ισάμην, beg

μητίετα, ὁ, counselor, deviser, *often an epithet of Zeus*

Μυρμιδόνες, -όνων, Myrmidons

ὄθομαι, + *gen.*, not to care for, care nothing for, *always appears with negative*

ὁμοιόω, ——, ——, ——, ——, ὡμοιώθην, liken oneself to; *in pass.*, be compared

στυγέω, ——, ἔστυξα, dread; hesitate

φέρτερος, -η, -ον, stronger

Φοῖβος, -ου, ὁ, Phoebus, *epithet of Apollo*

Χρυσηΐς, -ΐδος, ἡ, Chryseis

Notes

172 τόν: = αὐτόν

173 μάλ᾽: adds emphasis to the preceding imperat., "well then . . ."

174 εἵνεκ᾽ ἐμεῖο: Attic = ἐμοῦ ἕνεκα

πάρ᾽: The accent is critical: πάρα (not παρά) stands for πάρεστι, or as here, πάρεισι. The subj. is ἄλλοι.

174–75 καὶ ἄλλοι . . . μάλιστα δέ: "others also" sounds odd here, but it anticipates the most important member of the group to honor Agamemnon: Zeus

175 κέ: often used with the fut. tense to indicate a condition or place a limit. So here, "in that case, there are others who would honor me."

μητίετα: rare 1st declension masc., here with nom. sing. -α in place of -ης

176 ἔχθιστος: superl. < ἐχθρός

ἐσσι: 2nd sing. pres. indic. < εἰμί

178 τό: = αὐτό, another article used as a pron.

179 ἰών: pple. < εἶμι

180 Μυρμιδόνεσσιν: Verbs of ruling, such as ἀνάσσω, can be followed either by a dat., as here, or a gen.

σέθεν: gen. < σύ

181 οὐδ᾽ ὄθομαι κοτέοντος: Observe the force of the pres. pple., "I care nothing for your growing resentment."

182 ὥς: "just as . . ."

ἀφαιρεῖται: Note the force of the mid.

183 τήν: = αὐτήν

184 ἄγω: Homer uses subjnc. + κε to indicate the fut.

καλλιπάρῃον: Remember, compound adjs. do not have separate fem. endings.

185 αὐτός: emphatic, agreeing with subj., "I myself"

κλισίηνδε: The final **-δε** indicates motion toward. This suffix can be added to any substantive.

εἰδῇς: subjnc. < οἶδα

186   σέθεν: gen. of comparison

στυγέῃ: subjnc. again, after **ὄφρα**

187   φάσθαι: < φημί

ὁμοιωθήμεναι: aor. pass. infin. < ὁμοιόω

Summary

Agamemnon responds that Zeus will honor him, and that he does not need Achilles. Indeed he finds Achilles hateful for taking delight in battle. Agamemnon tells him to take his troops and go home.

Making Sense of It

τὸν δ(ὲ) ἠμείβετ(ο) ἔπειτα ἄναξ ἀνδρῶν Ἀγαμέμνων·

"φεῦγε μάλ(α), εἴ τοι θυμὸς ἐπέσσυται, οὐδέ σ(ε) ἔγωγε

λίσσομαι εἵνεκ(α) ἐμεῖο μένειν· πάρ(εισιν) ἔμοιγε καὶ ἄλλοι

175   οἵ κέ με τιμήσουσι, μάλιστα δὲ μητίετα Ζεύς.

ἔχθιστος δέ μοί ἐσσι διοτρεφέων βασιλήων·

αἰεὶ γάρ τοι ἔρις τέ (ἐστι) φίλη πόλεμοί τε μάχαι τε·

εἰ μάλα καρτερός ἐσσι, θεός που σοὶ τό γ(ε) ἔδωκεν·

οἴκαδ(ε) ἰὼν σὺν νηυσί τε σῇς καὶ σοῖς ἑτάροισι

180   Μυρμιδόνεσσιν ἄνασσε, **σέθεν** δ(ὲ) ἐγὼ οὐκ ἀλεγίζω,

οὐδ(ὲ) ὄθομαι **κοτέοντος**· ἀπειλήσω δὲ τοι ὧδε·

ὡς ἔμ(ε) ἀφαιρεῖται Χρυσηΐδα Φοῖβος Ἀπόλλων,

τὴν **μὲν** ἐγὼ σὺν νηΐ τ(ε) ἐμῇ καὶ ἐμοῖς ἑτάροισι

πέμψω, ἐγὼ **δέ** κ(ε) ἄγω Βρισηΐδα καλλιπάρηον

185   αὐτὸς ἰὼν κλισίηνδε, τὸ σὸν γέρας, ὄφρ(α) ἐῢ εἰδῇς

ὅσσον φέρτερός εἰμι σέθεν, **στυγέῃ** δὲ καὶ ἄλλος

ἶσον ἐμοὶ **φάσθαι** καὶ ὁμοιωθήμεναι ἄντην."

WHAT HOMER ACTUALLY COMPOSED

Vocabulary

ἀλεγίζω, have regard for, + *gen.*

ἄντην, face to face, openly against

ἀπειλέω, ἀπειλήσω, ἠπείλησα, declare; promise

Ἀπόλλων, -ωνος, ὁ, Apollo

ἀφαιρέω, ἀφαιρήσω, ἀφεῖλον, take away

Βρισηΐς, -ΐδος, ἡ, Briseis

γέρας, -αος, τό, prize of honor

διοτρεφής, -ές, cherished by Zeus

ἐπισσεύω, ——, ἐπέσ(σ)ευα, ——, ἐπέσ(σ)υμαι, ἐπεσ(σ)ύθην, set upon; *in pass.*, be eager, be incited

ἔρις, -ιδος, ἡ, strife

ἐχθρός, -ή, -όν, hateful to, + *dat.*

Ζεύς, Διός, ὁ, Zeus

ἴσος, -η, -ον, equal to, + *dat.*

καλλιπάρῃος, -ον, fair-cheeked

καρτερός, -ά, -όν, physically strong, powerful

κοτέω, ——, ἐκότεσ(σ)α, κεκότη(κ)α, resent, be angry at

λίσσομαι, ——, ἐλ(λ)ισάμην, beg

μητίετα, ὁ, counselor, deviser, *often an epithet of Zeus*

Μυρμιδόνες, -όνων, Myrmidons

ὄθομαι, + *gen.*, not to care for, care nothing for, *always appears with negative*

ὁμοιόω, ——, ——, ——, ——, ὡμοιώθην, liken oneself to; *in pass.*, be compared

στυγέω, ——, ἔστυξα, dread; hesitate

φέρτερος, -η, -ον, stronger

Φοῖβος, -ου, ὁ, Phoebus, *epithet of Apollo*

Χρυσηΐς, -ΐδος, ἡ, Chryseis

Notes

173–74 Note the word order. The juxtaposition of σ᾽ and ἔγωγε in the final position of line 173, followed by λίσσομαι in first position (ENJAMBMENT) in line 174, makes a very emphatic statement.

173–75 Agamemnon's acceptance of Achilles' threat to withdraw displays his shortsightedness and his misguided focus on his own personal honor. He is just as angry as Achilles at this point and his actions will have devastating consequences for his troops.

176–78 These lines demonstrate well Homer's ability to clarify and deepen the picture of a character in just a few lines. He is a master at delineating personality through the eyes of other characters.

179 Note the CHIASMUS in this line, and in line 183 in the same position.

181–87 Agamemnon reveals the shallowness of his thinking. He seems incapable of understanding the potential impact of his words and deeds. Homer shows us his excited state of mind in the metrics of these lines. For example, note the very early caesura and "bumpy" meter in 184. Look for other examples of peculiar scansion.

As It Was

τὸν δ' ἠμείβετ' ἔπειτα ἄναξ ἀνδρῶν Ἀγαμέμνων·

"φεῦγε μάλ', εἴ τοι θυμὸς ἐπέσσυται, οὐδέ σ' ἔγωγε

λίσσομαι εἴνεκ' ἐμεῖο μένειν· πάρ' ἔμοιγε καὶ ἄλλοι

175   οἵ κέ με τιμήσουσι, μάλιστα δὲ μητίετα Ζεύς.

ἔχθιστος δέ μοί ἐσσι διοτρεφέων βασιλήων·

αἰεὶ γάρ τοι ἔρις τε φίλη πόλεμοί τε μάχαι τε·

εἰ μάλα καρτερός ἐσσι, θεός που σοὶ τό γ' ἔδωκεν·

οἴκαδ' ἰὼν σὺν νηυσί τε σῆς καὶ σοῖς ἑτάροισι

180   Μυρμιδόνεσσιν ἄνασσε, σέθεν δ' ἐγὼ οὐκ ἀλεγίζω,

οὐδ' ὄθομαι κοτέοντος· ἀπειλήσω δέ τοι ὧδε·

ὡς ἔμ' ἀφαιρεῖται Χρυσηΐδα Φοῖβος Ἀπόλλων,

τὴν μὲν ἐγὼ σὺν νηΐ τ' ἐμῇ καὶ ἐμοῖς ἑτάροισι

πέμψω, ἐγὼ δέ κ' ἄγω Βρισηΐδα καλλιπάρηον

185   αὐτὸς ἰὼν κλισίηνδε, τὸ σὸν γέρας, ὄφρ' ἐῢ εἰδῇς

ὅσσον φέρτερός εἰμι σέθεν, στυγέῃ δὲ καὶ ἄλλος

ἶσον ἐμοὶ φάσθαι καὶ ὁμοιωθήμεναι ἄντην."

AFTER READING WHAT HOMER COMPOSED

1. How has Homer kept the theme of anger vivid in our mind's eye throughout these past few passages?

2. Would you say that Agamemnon's response here is calculated to provoke Achilles? Why or why not? Support your answer from the text!

3. Note the position of the pronouns at the end of line 173. Do you think the arrangement is significant? Why or why not?

READING 7

Paris Arms for a Duel with Menelaus

(*Iliad* 3.328–39)

Before You Read What Homer Composed

Introduction

Homeric epic is built around *formulae*, traditional phrases that occupy certain metrical positions within the hexameter, fill out an entire line, or even an entire formulaic scene. Whole passages may be repeated almost verbatim with minor variations, omissions, or expansions to fit the immediate context. Such repetitions may have allowed the poet to free his mind to compose the coming scene while maintaining the flow of the story according to audience expectations.

Common formulaic scenes include the various stages of dining, sacrifice, prayer, departure, and even the back and forth flow of battle. This reading features a typical arming scene, in which a hero puts on his armor in preparation for battle.

Keep This Grammar in Mind — Prepositions

As you well know, Greek grammar is supported by a complex system of prepositional phrases. In the passage below are several prepositions governing the dative case. Let's review this construction briefly.

In English, most uses of the dative case have been subsumed under the prepositions *to* or *for*. If you have studied Latin, you know that the dative had broad capabilities, yet was never directly used with prepositions. In Greek, however, many prepositions can govern the dative case:

Prepositions with the Dative (as well as the Genitive or Accusative)

ἀμφί	ἀνά	ἐπί	μετά
παρά	περί	ποτί / πρός	ὑπό

Prepositions with the Dative (exclusively)

ἐν(ί) / εἰν	σύν

We tend to think of the dative in terms of *location*, of being *in a particular place*. But the dative can also indicate the end result of some movement *toward* or *near* a particular place. The English preposition nearest to this sense of the dative is *upon*, now seldom used in American English. In the sentence, "he threw the scepter upon the ground," the expression "upon the ground," appears in the dative case, ποτὶ γαίη. Watch for the impression of completed motion accompanying the prepositional use of the dative as you read the arming scene.

Stopping for Some Practice — PREPOSITIONS

Read each sentence for meaning. Then, keeping in mind the grammar review, write a translation for each highlighted word or phrase. Take special note of the relationship between the word or phrase and the verb.

1. αὐτὰρ ὅ γ᾽ **ἀμφ᾽ ὤμοισιν** ἐδύσετο τεύχεα καλά.

   ―――――――――――

   Explain why **ἀμφ᾽** is shortened, or elided.

2. κνημῖδας μὲν πρῶτα **περὶ κνήμῃσιν** ἔθηκε.

   ―――――――――――

3. θώρηκα **περὶ στήθεσσιν** ἔδυνεν / . . . ἥρμοσε (< ἁρμόζω) δ᾽ **αὐτῷ**.

   ―――――――――――

   What preposition seems to be missing before **αὐτῷ**?

4. **κρατὶ** δ᾽ **ἔπ᾽ ἰφθίμῳ** κυνέην εὔτυκτον ἔθηκεν.

   ―――――――――――

   What is noteworthy about the arrangement of the prepositional phrase in this sentence? Refer to Appendix A on figures of speech (pp. 108–13). What is the name of such word order?

HELPING YOU READ WHAT HOMER COMPOSED

Vocabulary

Ἀλέξανδρος, -ου, ὁ, Alexander, i.e., Paris

ἄλκιμος, -η, -ον, strong

ἀραρίσκω, —, ἦρσα, ἄρηρα, —, ἤρθην, join,
    fit close

ἀργύρεος, -η, -ον, made of silver

ἀργυρόηλος, -η, -ον, studded with silver nails

ἀρήϊος, -ον, warlike

ἁρμόζω, —, ἥρμοσα, fit well

αὔτως, so, in this way

δεινός, -ή, -όν, terrible, dreadful

δεύτερος, -η, -ον, second

Ἑλένη, -ης, ἡ, Helen

ἔντεα, -ων, τά, armor

ἐπισφυρία, -ων, τά, bands, clasps for greaves

εὔτυκτος, -ον, well made

ἠΰκομος, -ον, with beautiful hair, *here an epithet of
    Helen*

θώρηξ, -ηκος, ὁ, breastplate

ἵππουρις, -ιδος, crested with horse hair

ἴφθιμος, -ον, strong, brave

καθύπερθε(ν), down from above

κάρη, κρατός, τό, head

κασιγήτος, -ου, ὁ, brother

κνήμη, -ης, ἡ, shin

κνημίς, -ίδος, ἡ, greaves

κυνέη, -ης, ἡ, helmet

λόφος, -ου, ὁ, crest

Λυκάων, -ωνος, ὁ, Lykaon, son of Priam

Μενέλαος, -ου, ὁ, Menelaus

νεύω, —, ἔνευσα, nod

ξίφος, εος, τό, sword

παλάμη, -ης, ἡ, hand

παλάμηφι(ν), *locative,* in the hand

πόσις, -ιος, ὁ, husband

σάκος, -εος, τό, shield

στιβαρός, -ή, -όν, heavy, stout

χάλκεος, -ον, made of bronze

Notes

328 **ὅ:** accent from the enclitic; definite article used as pron., referring to Paris/Alexander

ἐδύσετο: variant aor.; the mid. voice emphasizes both the reflexive nature of the action and its inherent interest to the subj.

330 **πρῶτα:** acc. neut. pl. used as adv.

ἔθηκε: aor. < τίθημι

331 **ἐπισφυρίοις:** dat. of instrument/means

ἀραρυίας: pf. pple. < ἀραρίσκω

333 **οἷο:** Attic = οὗ; in Homer, rel. prons. also function as demonstratives, here, in essence, "his"

ἥρμοσε: here, intransitive; understand θώρηξ as the subj.

αὐτῷ: i.e., Paris

336 **κρατί:** < κάρη

κρατὶ δ᾽ ἔπ᾽: A two-syllable prep. is accented on the first syllable if the noun obj. *precedes* it.

337 **ἵππουριν:** acc. < ἵππουρις

δεινόν: acc. neut. sing. used as adv.

338 **ἀρήρει:** plpf. < ἀραρίσκω

As You Read

1. What specific words signal the order of the series of events in the arming scene?

2. Does the hero arm from the head down, or the feet up? Why would that be so?

3. Identify the three prepositions that appear more than once in these lines. Why should they show up so often?

4. What two verbs are alternately used to capture the action as Paris dresses for battle?

5. Within the context, what is the effect of the use of CHIASMUS in line 331?

6. What part of speech is the form αὐτῷ in line 333? What is its case and its use?

Summary

A prominent part of the preparation for battle consists of putting on armor. In the *Iliad,* there are four full formulaic arming scenes, each with only minor variations. The heroes always put on their pieces of armor in the same order and Homer describes each scene with much the same vocabulary.

In this scene, Menelaus and Paris (here called Alexander) have agreed to fight a duel to determine the outcome of the war. Both sides are tired of the fighting and, since the argument is essentially between these two men (both of whom want Helen), the heroes are prepared to arm and fight to the death. In this passage Homer describes Paris donning his armor, and leaves Menelaus a single line to do the same.

From this point on, where the particles δε and γε are abbreviated (δ᾽, γ᾽), they will not be filled out.

Making Sense of It

αὐτὰρ ὅ γ᾽ ἀμφ(ὶ) ὤμοισιν ἐδύσετο τεύχεα καλὰ

δῖος Ἀλέξανδρος, **Ἑλένης** πόσις **ἠϋκόμοιο.**

330 **κνημῖδας** μὲν πρῶτα περὶ κνήμῃσιν ἔθηκε

καλάς, ἀργυρέοισιν ἐπισφυρίοις **ἀραρυίας·**

δεύτερον αὖ θώρηκα περὶ στήθεσσιν ἔδυνεν

οἷο κασιγνήτοιο Λυκάονος, (θώρηξ) ἥρμοσε δ᾽ αὐτῷ.

ἀμφὶ δ᾽ ἄρ(α) ὤμοισιν βάλετο **ξίφος ἀργυρόηλον**

335 **χάλκεον,** αὐτὰρ ἔπειτα σάκος μέγα τε στιβαρόν τε

κρατὶ δ᾽ ἐπ(ὶ) **ἰφθίμῳ** κυνέην εὔτυκτον ἔθηκεν

ἵππουριν· δεινὸν δὲ λόφος καθύπερθεν ἔνευεν·

εἵλετο δ᾽ **ἄλκιμον ἔγχος,** ὅ οἱ παλάμηφιν ἀρήρει.

ὣς δ᾽ αὔτως Μενέλαος ἀρήϊος ἔντε(α) ἔδυνεν.

What Homer Actually Composed

Vocabulary

Ἀλέξανδρος, -ου, ὁ, Alexander, i.e., Paris

ἄλκιμος, -η, -ον, strong

ἀραρίσκω, —, ἦρσα, ἄρηρα, —, ἤρθην, join, fit close

ἀργύρεος, -η, -ον, made of silver

ἀργυρόηλος, -η, -ον, studded with silver nails

ἀρήϊος, -ον, warlike

ἁρμόζω, —, ἥρμοσα, fit well

αὔτως, so, in this way

δεινός, -ή, -όν, terrible, dreadful

δεύτερος, -η, -ον, second

Ἑλένη, -ης, ἡ, Helen

ἔντεα, -ων, τά, armor

ἐπισφυρία, -ων, τά, bands, clasps for greaves

εὔτυκτος, -ον, well made

ἠΰκομος, -ον, with beautiful hair, *here an epithet of Helen*

θώρηξ, θώρηκος, ὁ, breastplate

ἵππουρις, -ιδος, crested with horse hair

ἴφθιμος, -ον, strong, brave

καθύπερθε(ν), down from above

κάρη, κρατός, τό, head

κασιγνήτος, -ου, ὁ, brother

κνήμη, -ης, ἡ, shin

κνημίς, -ίδος, ἡ, greaves

κυνέη, -ης, ἡ, helmet

λόφος, -ου, ὁ, crest

Λυκάων, -ωνος, ὁ, Lykaon, son of Priam

Μενέλαος, -ου, ὁ, Menelaus

νεύω, —, ἔνευσα, nod

ξίφος, -εος, τό, sword

παλάμη, -ης, ἡ, hand

παλάμηφι(ν), *locative,* in the hand

πόσις, -ιος, ὁ, husband

σάκος, -εος, τό, shield

στιβαρός, -ή, -όν, heavy, stout

χάλκεος, -ον, made of bronze

Notes

329   Note that Helen's name rests neatly in the center of the line, with six syllables before it and seven following. What is the effect?

330   The arming begins with the greaves, although the initial statement tells us that Paris put his armor around his shoulders. There is a practical reason to begin with the greaves; if the warrior had the rest of his armor on, it would be difficult to put on the shin guards.

334   Greek weapons and armor from Bronze Age graves notable for their material wealth include greaves, helmets, breastplates, and silver-studded swords, some bearing elaborate scenes of war or the hunt.

As You Read

1.   Explain *two* dialectic characteristics in the form ἠΰκόμοιο, found in line 329.

2.   Explain the form οἶο in line 333. What would its Attic form be?

3.   Based on the variation in dialects available to Homer, what decision has the poet made in adopting the forms ἥρμοσε, ἔδυνεν, and ἐδύσετο? Why might the poet have preferred these forms?

As It Was

αὐτὰρ ὅ γ᾽ ἀμφ᾽ ὤμοισιν ἐδύσετο τεύχεα καλὰ

δῖος Ἀλέξανδρος, Ἑλένης πόσις ἠϋκόμοιο.

330 κνημῖδας μὲν πρῶτα περὶ κνήμῃσιν ἔθηκε

καλάς, ἀργυρέοισιν ἐπισφυρίοις ἀραρυίας·

δεύτερον αὖ θώρηκα περὶ στήθεσσιν ἔδυνεν

οἶο κασιγνήτοιο Λυκάονος· ἥρμοσε δ᾽ αὐτῷ.

ἀμφὶ δ᾽ ἄρ᾽ ὤμοισιν βάλετο ξίφος ἀργυρόηλον

335 χάλκεον, αὐτὰρ ἔπειτα σάκος μέγα τε στιβαρόν τε

κρατὶ δ᾽ ἐπ᾽ ἰφθίμῳ κυνέην εὔτυκτον ἔθηκεν

ἵππουριν· δεινὸν δὲ λόφος καθύπερθεν ἔνευεν·

εἵλετο δ᾽ ἄλκιμον ἔγχος, ὅ οἱ παλάμηφιν ἀρήρει.

ὣς δ᾽ αὔτως Μενέλαος ἀρήιος ἔντε᾽ ἔδυνεν.

AFTER READING WHAT HOMER COMPOSED

1. The ritual of arming for war as described in this passage is reflected in modern cultures, not necessarily within the context of war. How does each of the following find a parallel in the arming scene in Book 3?

    - A batter at the plate or in the on-deck circle
    - A catcher putting on his equipment before taking the field
    - Preparation for a wedding
    - Fans preparing to attend a football game or soccer match

2. Can you imagine how Homer's description in this reading could be helpful to an archaeologist? Conduct an online image search for one or more of the following:

    - An ancient *Greek vase painting* showing a warrior dressing for battle
    - A *Mycenaean "warrior krater"*
    - A suit of *Greek Bronze Age armor*

3. Why do you suppose Homer's audience liked the recurrent arming scenes? Can you think of any arming scenes in "The Matrix" (1999) or other films that might draw on the same sort of feelings?

READING 8

Diomedes Displays His Prowess in Battle

(*Iliad* 5.297–317)

BEFORE YOU READ WHAT HOMER COMPOSED

Introduction

Aeneas, later the hero of Vergil's first-century BCE Latin epic, the *Aeneid*, makes several appearances in the *Iliad*. In the following selection Aeneas is assaulted by Diomedes while guarding the shattered corpse of the Trojan hero Pandarus, a victim of Diomedes' spear. Aeneas barely escapes death, and he does so only through divine agency.

Dealing With Dialect — FURTHER DIALECT VARIANTS

In the following passage, there are several variant forms attributable to the influence of regional dialects. Ionic Greek is evident, for instance, in the aorist middle optative ἐρυσαίατο, which in Attic would appear as ἐρύσαιντο:

> δείσας μή πώς οἱ **ἐρυσαίατο** νεκρὸν Ἀχαιοί.
> " . . . fearing lest somehow the Achaeans would drag the body from him."

The genitive singular ending -οιο, which appears in the noun πέπλοιο, is actually a dialect form found as early as the Bronze Age Linear B tablets:

> πρόσθε δέ οἱ **πέπλοιο φαεινοῦ** πτύγμ᾽ ἐκάλυψεν.
> "She wrapped around him the fold of her shining robe."

As you encounter these dialectical variants, you will naturally become accustomed to them, just as you might read Dickens' "flavour" as "flavor" without conscious visual adjustment.

Keep This Grammar in Mind — Dual Nouns

In addition to singular and plural endings, Greek has separate forms to mark a group of two. These forms, called duals, are generally used for items that come naturally in pairs, e.g., eyes or hands, but they can indicate two of anything.

	Dual Endings		
	1st Declension	2nd Declension	3rd Declension
Nom. / Acc. / Voc.	-α Ἀτρείδα	-ω πέπλω	-ε ἄνδρε
Gen. / Dat.	-ῃιν Ἀτρείδῃιν	-οιιν πέπλοιιν	-οιιν ἀνδροῖιν

Stopping for Some Practice — Dual Nouns

Study each sentence and identify all dual forms.

1. ὁ δὲ χερμάδιον λάβε χειρὶ / . . . ὃ οὐ δύο γ᾽ ἄνδρε φέροιεν.

2. πρὸς δ᾽ ἄμφω ῥῆξε τένοντε.

3. ἀμφὶ δὲ ὄσσε κελαινὴ νὺξ ἐκάλυψε.

4. ἀμφὶ δ᾽ ἑὸν φίλον υἱὸν ἐχεύατο πήχεε λευκώ.

HELPING YOU READ WHAT HOMER COMPOSED

Vocabulary

Αἰνείας, -αο, ὁ, Aeneas

ἀλκή, -ῆς, ἡ, strength

ἀπορούω, ——, ἀπόρουσα, spring, dart off

ἀσπίς, -ίδος, ἡ, shield

Ἀχαιοί, -ῶν, οἱ, Achaeans

ἔϊσος, -η, -ον, well-balanced

ἐνστρέφω, turn inside of

ἐρύω, ἐρύω, εἴρυσα, ——, εἴρυσμαι, draw away, drag

ἰάχω, shout

ἰσχίον, -ου, τό, hip socket

κοτύλη, -ης, ἡ, cup; socket

λέων, -οντος, ὁ, lion

μακρός, -ή, -όν, long

μέμαα, *only in pf.,* be eager

μηρός, -οῦ, ὁ, thigh

νεκρός, -οῦ, ὁ, corpse

πάλλω, ——, ἔπηλα, shake, brandish; hurl

πάντοσε, in all directions

πρόσθε, before, in front of

ῥέα, easily

σμερδαλέα, loudly

Τυδεΐδης, -ου, ὁ, Diomedes, son of Tydeus

χερμάδιον, -ου, τό, large stone

Notes

298 **δείσας μή:** Subordinate clauses, here a fearing clause, need not be introduced by a conjugated verb. What form is **δείσας** (< δείδω)?

οἷ: dat. sing. pron. referring to Aeneas; not nom. pl. with Ἀχαιοί

ἐρυσαίατο: Homeric 3ʳᵈ pl. aor. mid. < ἐρύω

299 **λέων ὥς:** An unaccented ὡς would normally precede λέων rather than follow.

βαῖνε: It might help to repeat the verb, "he went as a lion *would go* . . . "

ἀλκί, = ἀλκῇ

πεποιθώς: pf. pple. < πείθω, "trusting in . . . "

301 **κτάμεναι:** aor. act. infin. < κτείνω

μεμαώς: pf. act. pple., translate as pres.

τοῦ: = αὐτοῦ, i.e., Aeneas

ἔλθοι: indefinite rel. clauses follow the pattern set by conditionals

303 **Τυδεΐδης:** Diomedes is referred to by his patronym as the son of Tydeus.

μέγα ἔργον: in apposition with χερμάδιον λάβε

φέροιεν: potential opt.; in Attic this would be accompanied by ἄν

304 **οἵοι . . . οἷος:** The breathing marks are crucial to distinguish the two words.

μιν: i.e., the stone

καί: adverbial, "even (though) . . . "

305 **τῷ:** "with this (stone) he struck . . . "

Αἰνείαο: Homeric gen. sing.

As You Read

1. Why does the optative appear in line 301? With what conjunction could you replace ὅς τις to test your answer?

2. Lines 305–308 are difficult to translate, given their graphic portrayal of the brutality of hand-to-hand combat. How do these lines affect you?

3. What dialect variants do you spot in the reading?

Summary

Aeneas and Pandarus have mounted Aeneas' chariot and are racing to challenge Diomedes, who relishes not only the prospect of defeat for the two Trojans, but also the securing of Aeneas' horses as prizes. Pandarus makes the first strike, piercing Diomedes' shield but missing the warrior. Diomedes' retaliatory spear horribly and fatally wounds Pandarus, a full strike to the face.

The reading takes up the story at this point. Lion-like, Aeneas leaps from the chariot to stand over his fallen comrade, guarding his body from the plunderers. Thus distracted, Aeneas is struck by a huge stone hurled by Diomedes.

Aphrodite enters the conflict and shields her son Aeneas. The reading ends at this point, but the action continues in Reading 9 as Diomedes wounds Aphrodite with a spear thrust and Aeneas is spirited away by Apollo.

Making Sense of It

You should be able to recognize elisions of ἄρα and τε by now, so their full forms will no longer be provided.

> Αἰνείας δ᾽ ἀπόρουσε σὺν ἀσπίδι δουρί τε μακρῷ,
>
> δείσας μή πώς οἱ ἐρυσαίατο νεκρὸν Ἀχαιοί.
>
> ἀμφὶ δ᾽ ἄρ᾽ αὐτῷ βαῖνε λέων ὣς ἀλκὶ πεποιθώς,
>
> 300   πρόσθε δέ οἱ δόρυ τ᾽ ἔσχε καὶ ἀσπίδα πάντοσ(ε) ἐΐσην,
>
> τὸν κτάμεναι μεμαὼς ὅς τις τοῦ γ᾽ ἀντίος ἔλθοι,
>
> σμερδαλέα ἰάχων· ὁ δὲ χερμάδιον λάβε χειρὶ
>
> Τυδεΐδης, μέγα ἔργον, ὃ οὐ δύο γ᾽ ἄνδρε φέροιεν,
>
> οἷοι νῦν βροτοί εἰσ(ι)· ὁ δέ μιν ῥέα πάλλε καὶ οἶος.
>
> 305   τῷ βάλεν Αἰνείαο κατ(ὰ) ἰσχίον, ἔνθα τε μηρὸς
>
> ἰσχίῳ ἐνστρέφεται, κοτύλην δέ τέ μιν καλέουσι

Vocabulary

Ἀγχίσης, -αο, ὁ, Anchises

Αἰνείας, -αο, ὁ, Aeneas

ἀντίος, -η, -ον, + *gen.,* opposite, against

Ἀφροδίτη, -ης, ἡ, Aphrodite

βέλος, -εος, τό, missile

βουκολέω, tend cattle

γνύξ, on bended knee

Δαναοί, -ῶν, οἱ, Danaans

ἐρείδω, ——, ἔρεισα, ——, ἐρηρέδαμαι, prop up,
   push; *in mid.,* lean, + *gen.*

ἐρείπω, ——, ἤριπα, pull down; *in mid.,* fall

ἕρκος, -εος, τό, barrier

Ζεύς, Διός, ὁ, Zeus

θλάω, ——, ἔθλασ(σ)α, smash, crush

θυγάτηρ, -τρός, ἡ, daughter

κελαινός, -ή, -όν, dark, black

λευκός, -ή, -όν, white

λίθος, -ου, ὁ, stone

ὀξύς, -εῖα, -ύ, sharp

ὄσσε, *dual,* eyes

παχύς, -εῖα, -ύ, thick

πέπλος, -ου, ὁ, robe

πῆχυς, -εος, ὁ, forearm

πτύγμα, -ατος, τό, folds of cloth

ῥήγνυμι, ῥήξω, ἔρηξα, break

ῥινόν, -οῦ, τό, skin, hide

ταχύπωλος, -ον, with swift horses

τένων, -οντος, ὁ, tendon

τρηχύς, -εῖα, -ύ, rough

φαεινός, -ή, -όν, shining

ὠθέω, ——, ὦσα, push, thrust

Notes

309   γνύξ: occurs only in this phrase in Homer, "falling (ἐριπών) on bended knee (γνύξ)"

310   γαίης: partit. gen., "leaned upon (a part of) the ground"

311   νύ κεν ἔνθ᾽ ἀπόλοιτο: mixed condition using an aor. in the dependent clause and an opt. in the main clause; "he would have perished, had not Aphrodite . . . "

312   ὀξύ: adverbial, as neut. acc. forms often are

313   τέκε: < τίκτω

314   ἐχεύατο: < χέω, "pour her arms around" = "embrace"; asigmatic aors. are frequent in Homer

   πήχεε λευκώ: acc. dual; πῆχυς generally means *forearm,* but by SYNECDOCHE here it stands for the whole arm.

315   οἱ: dative of advantage.

   πρόσθε: adverbial here.

316   ἔμεν: infin. < εἰμί, one of many Homeric forms (see p. 9)

   μή: Negative purpose clauses may be introduced by μή alone.

317   ἕλοιτο: aor. opt. (in secondary sequence) < αἱρέω

   ἐκ: Homer frequently uses preps. as bare advs.; translate as though prefixed to the verb (see TMESIS).

Making Sense of It (Continued)

θλάσσε δέ οἱ κοτύλην, πρὸς δ᾽ **ἄμφω** ῥῆξε **τένοντε·**

ὦσε δ᾽ ἀπὸ ῥινὸν τρηχὺς λίθος· αὐτὰρ ὁ γ᾽ ἥρως

ἔστη γνὺξ ἐριπὼν καὶ ἐρείσατο **χειρὶ παχείῃ**

310   γαίης· ἀμφὶ δὲ ὄσσε κελαινὴ νὺξ ἐκάλυψε.

καί νύ κεν ἔνθ(α) ἀπόλοιτο ἄναξ ἀνδρῶν Αἰνείας,

εἰ μὴ ἄρ᾽ ὀξὺ **νόησε** Διὸς **θυγάτηρ Ἀφροδίτη**

μήτηρ, ἥ μιν ὑπ(ὸ) Ἀγχίσῃ τέκε βουκολέοντι·

ἀμφὶ δ᾽ ἑὸν φίλον υἱὸν ἐχεύατο πήχεε λευκώ,

315   πρόσθε δέ οἱ πέπλοιο φαεινοῦ πτύγμ(α) ἐκάλυψεν,

ἕρκυς ἔμεν βελέων, μή **τις** Δαναῶν ταχυπώλων

χαλκὸν ἐνὶ στήθεσσι **βαλὼν** ἐκ θυμὸν ἕλοιτο.

WHAT HOMER ACTUALLY COMPOSED

Vocabulary

Αἰνείας, -αο, ὁ, Aeneas

ἀλκή, -ῆς, ἡ, strength

ἀπορούω, ——, ἀπόρουσα, spring, dart off

ἀσπίς, -ίδος, ἡ, shield

Ἀχαιοί, -ῶν, οἱ, Achaeans

ἔϊσος, -η, -ον, well-balanced

ἐνστρέφω, turn inside of

ἐρύω, ἐρύω, εἴρυσα, ——, εἴρυσμαι, draw away, drag

ἰάχω, shout

ἰσχίον, -ου, τό, hip socket

κοτύλη, -ης, ἡ, cup; socket

λέων, -οντος, ὁ, lion

μακρός, -ή, -όν, long

μέμαα, *only in pf.,* be eager

μηρός, -οῦ, ὁ, thigh

νεκρός, -οῦ, ὁ, corpse

πάλλω, ——, ἔπηλα, shake, brandish; hurl

πάντοσε, in all directions

πρόσθε, before, in front of

ῥέα, easily

σμερδαλέα, loudly

Τυδεΐδης, -οῦ, ὁ, Diomedes, son of Tydeus

χερμάδιον, -ου, τό, large stone

Notes

299 Note that a SIMILE may be brief and still vivid. Observe also how λέων precedes ὥς by way of ANAS-TROPHE, leaving the line divided into three balanced metric units comprised of a dactyl followed by a spondee.

301 The antecedent of ὅς τις is τόν, used as a pronoun; note that it is removed from the indefinite pronoun, illustrative of Aeneas' placing himself between Pandarus' body and any enemies approaching to plunder it.

302–304 The image contained in these lines occurs several times elsewhere in the *Iliad*. The notion that men in the "old days" were tougher, stronger, greater than those in the current age remains a TOPOS of literature even today.

305 The second alpha in **Αἰνείαο** is a separate syllable and it is long. The word is thus four syllables, **Αἰ-νεί-α-ο.**"

306 The final syllable of **ἰσχίῳ** is shortened by correption, producing a fully dactylic line.

As It Was

Αἰνείας δ᾽ ἀπόρουσε σὺν ἀσπίδι δουρί τε μακρῷ,

δείσας μή πώς οἱ ἐρυσαίατο νεκρὸν Ἀχαιοί.

ἀμφὶ δ᾽ ἄρ᾽ αὐτῷ βαῖνε λέων ὣς ἀλκὶ πεποιθώς

300   πρόσθε δέ οἱ δόρυ τ᾽ ἔσχε καὶ ἀσπίδα πάντοσ᾽ ἐΐσην.

τὸν κτάμεναι μεμαὼς ὅς τις τοῦ γ᾽ ἀντίος ἔλθοι,

σμερδαλέα ἰάχων· ὁ δὲ χερμάδιον λάβε χειρὶ

Τυδεΐδης, μέγα ἔργον, ὃ οὐ δύο γ᾽ ἄνδρε φέροιεν,

οἷοι νῦν βροτοί εἰσ᾽· ὁ δέ μιν ῥέα πάλλε καὶ οἶος.

305   τῷ βάλεν Αἰνείαο κατ᾽ ἰσχίον, ἔνθα τε μηρὸς

ἰσχίῳ ἐνστρέφεται, κοτύλην δέ τέ μιν καλέουσι·

Vocabulary

Ἀγχίσης, -αο, ὁ, Anchises

Αἰνείας, -αο, ὁ, Aeneas

ἀντίος, -η, -ον, + gen., opposite, against

Ἀφροδίτη, -ης, ἡ, Aphrodite

βέλος, -εος, τό, missile

βουκολέω, tend cattle

γνύξ, on bended knee

Δαναοί, -ῶν, οἱ, Danaans

ἐρείδω, —, ἔρεισα, —, ἐρηρέδαμαι, prop up, push; in mid., lean, + gen.

ἐρείπω, —, ἤριπα, pull down; in mid., fall

ἕρκος, -εος, τό, barrier

Ζεύς, Διός, ὁ, Zeus

θλάω, —, ἔθλασ(σ)α, smash, crush

θυγάτηρ, -τρός, ἡ, daughter

κελαινός, -ή, -όν, dark, black

λευκός, -ή, -όν, white

λίθος, -ου, ὁ, stone

ὀξύς, -εῖα, -ύ, sharp

ὄσσε, dual, eyes

παχύς, -εῖα, -ύ, thick

πέπλος, -ου, ὁ, robe

πῆχυς, -εος, ὁ, forearm

πτύγμα, -ατος, τό, folds of cloth

ῥήγνυμι, ῥήξω, ἔρηξα, break

ῥινόν, -οῦ, τό, skin, hide

ταχύπωλος, -ον, with swift horses

τένων, -οντος, ὁ, tendon

τρηχύς, -εῖα, -ύ, rough

φαεινός, -ή, -όν, shining

ὠθέω, —, ὦσα, push, thrust

Notes

309–11   Note the ASSONANCE of ἔστη γνὺξ ... κελαινὴ νὺξ, followed by the REPETITION of ἐκάλυψε in lines 310 and 315; the gravity of the wound and its natural outcome is effectively contrasted with the hero's salvation.

δὲ (ϝ)ὄσσε: The hiatus may be attributed to an original initial digamma (ϝ) subsequently lost from Greek, but in effect preserved by the conservative structure of oral poetics. The digamma, representing the sound "w," can be detected in other words related to vision, such as the root seen in the aorist infinitive, (ϝ)ἰδεῖν; compare Latin *video*, which is from the same Indo-European root and has retained the "w."

310   γαίης: a nice example of ENJAMBMENT. The word falls more heavily on our ears for the delay, and we feel more fully the futile grasping of the earth, the attempt to cling to something of this world. Just as his hand is stretched, so is our attention as we wait for that final word to fall.

313:   Julius Caesar would claim divine ancestry by tracing his lineage back to Iulus, the son of Aeneas according to later tradition, and so the grandson of Aphrodite.

As It Was (Continued)

θλάσσε δέ οἱ κοτύλην, πρὸς δ᾿ ἄμφω ῥῆξε τένοντε·

ὦσε δ᾿ ἀπὸ ῥινὸν τρηχὺς λίθος· αὐτὰρ ὁ γ᾿ ἥρως

ἔστη γνὺξ ἐριπὼν καὶ ἐρείσατο χειρὶ παχείῃ

310 γαίης· ἀμφὶ δὲ ὄσσε κελαινὴ νὺξ ἐκάλυψε.

καί νύ κεν ἔνθ᾿ ἀπόλοιτο ἄναξ ἀνδρῶν Αἰνείας,

εἰ μὴ ἄρ᾿ ὀξὺ νόησε Διὸς θυγάτηρ Ἀφροδίτη

μήτηρ, ἥ μιν ὑπ᾿ Ἀγχίσῃ τέκε βουκολέοντι·

ἀμφὶ δ᾿ ἑὸν φίλον υἱὸν ἐχεύατο πήχεε λευκώ,

315 πρόσθε δέ οἱ πέπλοιο φαεινοῦ πτύγμ᾿ ἐκάλυψεν,

ἕρκος ἔμεν βελέων, μή τις Δαναῶν ταχυπώλων

χαλκὸν ἐνὶ στήθεσσι βαλὼν ἐκ θυμὸν ἕλοιτο.

AFTER READING WHAT HOMER COMPOSED

1. What common epic device is exemplified in the form Τυδεΐδης (line 303)?

   Research Tydeus. For what deeds is he known? Do you think this epic device enhances the role of the character referred to in this scene? In your experience, how do certain surnames from "modern" languages equate to the use of this device? Can you think of examples illustrating how notable figures can be exalted because of their ancestries?

2. Look back at the family relationships mentioned in 311–13. How does the participle βουκολέοντι set the tone for the background information provided in these lines? Research Aphrodite and Anchises, and draw a genealogical chart for Aphrodite based on these lines. Is the participle βουκολέοντι appropriate to the character of Anchises as understood elsewhere in the mythic tradition? What does this comparison suggest about the consistency of Greek myth?

   Reflect on the arrangement of the words in 312–13. Does this arrangement enhance your reading of the text? How?

READING 9

The Aristeia *of Diomedes Continued*

(*Iliad* 5.318–52)

BEFORE YOU READ WHAT HOMER COMPOSED

Introduction

This selection continues the previous Reading's scene taken from Diomedes' finest moment, or *aristeia*, which occupies Book 5. Aeneas is saved by his mother, Aphrodite, but not without surprising consequences. She discovers that the battlefield is not her place, and Diomedes earns a unique spot among heroes.

Keep This Grammar in Mind — THE VERB εἰμί

Keep in mind that εἰμί, "be," has only present, imperfect, and future tense forms. The imperfect in Homer often appears uncontracted. The future is deponent. There is no aorist, no perfect or pluperfect, and no future perfect. Here are the present, imperfect, and future tense forms in the indicative:

Present Tense

εἰμί	I am	εἰμέν	we are
ἐσσί	you are	ἐστέ	you (pl.) are
ἐστί	s/he is	εἰσί	they are

Imperfect Tense

ἦ(ν)	I was	ἦμεν	we were
ἦσθα	you were	ἦτε	you (pl.) were
ἦν / ἔην	s/he was	ἦσαν / ἔσαν	they were

Future Tense

ἔσομαι	I shall be	ἐσόμεθα	we shall be
ἔσει	you will be	ἔσεσθε	you (pl.) will be
ἔσται	s/he will be	ἔσονται	they will be

The infinitive, which you know as **εἶναι** in Attic, appears in Homer in several variants—for example, as ἔμεν (cf. p. 9).

The participles exist in the present and the future:

Present Tense

m.	*f.*	*n.*
ὤν / ἐών	οὖσα / ἐοῦσα	ὄν / ἐόν
ὄντος / **ἐόντος**	οὔσης / ἐούσης	ὄντος / **ἐόντος**
etc.		

Future Tense

m.	*f.*	*n.*
ἐσόμενος	ἐσομένη	ἐσόμενον
ἐσομένου	ἐσομένης	ἐσομένου
etc.		

Stopping for Some Practice — εἰμί

Study the following clauses. One you have seen before; the others will occur in this or a future reading. Note the tense and mood of **εἰμί** in each.

1. πρόσθε δέ οἱ πέπλοιο φαεινοῦ πτύγμ᾽ ἐκάλυψεν, / ἕρκος ἔμεν βελέων.

   Tense and Mood: _____

2. ὁ δὲ Κύπριν ἐπῴχετο νηλέϊ χαλκῷ, / γιγνώσκων ὅ τ᾽ ἄναλκις ἔην θεός.

   Tense and Mood: _____

3. οἳ δὲ μοι ἑπτὰ κασίγνητοι ἔσαν ἐν μεγάροισιν, / οἱ μὲν πάντες ἰῷ κίον ἤματι Ἄϊδος εἴσω.

   Tense and Mood: _____

4. Ἕκτορ, ἀτὰρ σύ μοί ἐσσι πατὴρ καὶ πότνια μήτηρ / ἠδὲ κασίγνητος, σὺ δέ μοι θαλερὸς παρακοίτης.

   Tense and Mood: _____

5. . . . τοῖος ἐὼν οἷος οὔ τις Ἀχαιῶν χαλκοχιτώνων / ἐν πολέμῳ· ἀγορῇ δέ τ᾽ ἀμείνονές εἰσι καὶ ἄλλοι.

   Tense and Mood: _____; _____

HELPING YOU READ WHAT HOMER COMPOSED

Vocabulary

Ἀθηναίη, -ης, ἡ, Athena

Αἰνείας, -αο, ὁ, Aeneas

ἄντυξ, -υγος, ὁ, front rail of a chariot; shield rim

Ἀχαιοί, -ῶν, οἱ, Achaeans

Δηΐπυλος, -ου, ὁ, Deipylus

Διομήδης, -ους, ὁ, Diomedes

ἐμμεμαώς, -υια, eager

Ἐνυω, -οῦς, ἡ, Enyo

ἐρύκω, —, ἔρυξα / ἠρύκακα, hold back, restrain

καλλίθριξ, καλλίτριχος, with beautiful hair

Καπανεύς, -ῆος, ὁ, Kapaneus

Κύπρις, -ιδος, ἡ, Cypris, i.e., Aphrodite

λανθάνω, λήσω, ἔλαθον, —, λέλασμαι, escape notice; in mid., forget, + gen.

συνθεσίη, -ης, ἡ, in pl., covenant, instructions

Τρῶοι, -ων, οἱ, Trojans

Τυδεΐδης, -ου, ὁ, Diomedes, son of Tydeus

ὑπεκφέρω, carry away from, + gen.

Notes

318   ἥ: i.e., Aphrodite

319   υἱὸς Καπανῆος: Sthenelus

ἐλήθετο: impf. mid. < λήθω, a poetic form of λανθάνω

συνθεσιάων: In Book 5.259–73 Diomedes gives Sthenelus instructions to drive away to the Greek lines the famous horses of Aeneas. These were born from the horses given by Zeus to Tros in exchange for the theft of Ganymede.

320   τάων: uncontracted fem. gen. pl. of the demonstr. pron.

βοὴν ἀγαθός: the standard epithet for Diomedes, "great at shouting"

321   μώνυχας ἵππους: The declension combination -ας / -ους occurs again in lines 323–24 and elsewhere. Watch for it.

322   τείνας, aor. pple. < τείνω

324   ἐξέλασε: < ἐξελαύνω

325   δῶκε: aor. < δίδωμι

326   τίεν: < τίω

οἱ φρεσὶν ἄρτια: "things suited to his own (i.e., Sthenelus') heart"

ᾔδη: plpf. < οἶδα, translate as simple past

327   ἔπι: note the accent, indicating a preceding noun obj.

ἐλαυνέμεν: pres. act. infin. (see p. 9); the infin. explains why Sthenelus gave Deipylus the horses

ὅ γ᾽ ἥρως: i.e., Sthenelus

328   ὧν: reflex. adj.

ἐπιβάς: aor. pple. < ἐπιβαίνω

329   μέθεπε: takes double acc., "spurred his horses after Diomedes"

330   ὁ δέ: i.e., Diomedes

Κύπριν: acc. sing.

ἐπῴχετο: < ἐποίχομαι

χαλκῷ: referring by METONYMY to a blade made of bronze

331   ὅ τ᾽: "(the fact) that"; Homer often adds an untranslatable τε following a rel. pron., as also in the following line, αἵ τ᾽

ἔην: uncontracted impf. < εἰμί

θεάων: partit. gen.

332   τάων αἵ τ᾽: "those who . . ."

πόλεμον κάτα: The accent shifts when a two-syllable prep. follows its noun.

As You Read

1. To increase reading speed, learn well the Homeric pronouns and possessive adjectives, such as ἥ and ἑόν in the first line of this passage. Find as many of these as you can in this passage and identify their form and use.

2. The ability to recognize compound words and guess their meanings based on their roots will also speed up your reading. The words ὑπεξέφερεν (line 318) and καλλίτριχας (line 323) are two of the many compound words in this passage. Find others and see whether you can guess their meanings.

Summary

Diomedes' companion Sthenelus secures Aeneas' horses as a valuable war prize. Diomedes attacks and wounds Aphrodite. From her wound we learn something about the dining habits of the gods, and also about their stamina in warfare. Diomedes has harsh words for the goddess.

Making Sense of It

ἥ μὲν ἑὸν φίλον υἱὸν ὑπεξέφερεν πολέμοιο·

οὐδ᾽ υἱὸς Καπανῆος ἐλήθετο συνθεσιάων

320   τάων ἃς ἐπέτελλε βοὴν ἀγαθὸς Διομήδης,

ἀλλ(ὰ) ὅ γε τοὺς μὲν ἑοὺς ἠρύκακε **μώνυχας ἵππους**

νόσφιν ἀπὸ φλοίσβου, ἐξ ἄντυγος ἡνία ῑείνας,

Αἰνείαο δ᾽ ἐπαΐξας καλλίτριχας ἵππους

ἐξέλασε Τρώων μετ(ὰ) ἐϋκνήμιδας Ἀχαιούς.

325   δῶκε δὲ Δηϊπύλῳ, ἑτάρῳ φίλῳ, ὃν περὶ πάσης

τῖεν ὁμηλικίης, ὅτι οἱ φρεσὶν ἄρτια ᾔδη,

νηυσὶν ἔπι γλαφυρῇσιν ἐλαυνέμεν· αὐτὰρ ὅ γ᾽ ἥρως

ὧν ἵππων ἐπιβὰς ἔλαβ(ε) ἡνία σιγαλόεντα,

αἶψα δὲ Τυδεΐδην μέθεπε κρατερώνυχας ἵππους

330   ἐμμεμαώς· ὁ δὲ Κύπριν ἐπῴχετο νηλέϊ χαλκῷ,

γιγνώσκων ὅ τ᾽ ἄναλκις ἔην θεός, οὐδὲ θεάων

τάων αἵ τ᾽ ἀνδρῶν πόλεμον κάτα κοιρανέουσιν,

οὔτ᾽ ἄρ(α) Ἀθηναίη οὔτε **πτολίπορθος** Ἐνυώ.

Vocabulary

ἀλύω, be distressed

Ἀπόλλων, -ωνος, ὁ, Apollo

Δαναοί, -ῶν, οἱ, Danaans

Διομήδης, -ους, ὁ, Diomedes

ἐρύω, ἐρύω, εἴρυσα, ——, εἴρυσμαι, drag

Ζεύς, Διός, ὁ, Zeus

ἠπεροπεύω, deceive

θέναρ, -αρος, τό, palm of hand

καταβάλλω, ——, κατέβαλα, throw down, drop

πυνθάνομαι, πεύσομαι, ἐπυθόμην, ——, πέπυσμαι, learn by inquiry

Τυδεύς, -έος, ὁ, Tydeus

Φοῖβος, -ου, ὁ, Phoebus, *epithet of Apollo*

Χάριτες, -ων, αἱ, the Graces

Notes

336 μετάλμενος: < μεθάλλομαι

ὀξέϊ: dat. sing. < ὀξύς

338 οἱ: dat. fem. sing.

αὐταί: emphatic, "themselves"

339 πρυμνὸν ὕπερ θέναρος: "over the base of the hand," here = "wrist"; note the accent of the prep.

340 μακάρεσσι θεοῖσιν: "in the blessed gods"

341 ἔδουσ᾽: < ἐσθίω

342 τοὔνεκ᾽: = τοῦ ἕνεκα, "because of which (fact)"

ἀναίμονες: "bloodless"; ἀν- is a negative prefix on the root αἷμα, "blood"

καλέονται: pass. + predicate nom.

343 ἕο: reflex., gen. obj. of prep.

κάββαλεν: syncopated form < καταβάλλω

344 μετὰ χερσίν: "in his hands"

345 κυανέη νεφέλη: instrumental dat.

345–46 μὴ . . . ἕλοιτο: opt. in secondary sequence in place of the expected subjnc.; negative purpose clauses do not need a conjunction.

347 μακρόν: neut. acc. used as adv.

ἄϋσε: aor. < ἀϋω

349 οὐχ ἅλις [sc. ἐστί] ὅττι: "isn't it enough that . . . "

350 πωλήσεαι: fut. < πωλέομαι

350–51 ὀΐω: introduces the main clause in indir. statement, and the *if*-clause is governed by πύθηαι

351 καὶ εἴ: concessive, "even if . . . "

ἑτέρωθι: "from someone else"; Aphrodite will not be able even to hear reports about war

πύθηαι: aor. subjnc. < πυνθάνομαι

Making Sense of It (Continued)

ἀλλ(ὰ) ὅτε δή ῥ(α) ἐκίχανε πολὺν κατ(ὰ) ὅμιλον ὀπάζων,

335 ἔνθ᾽ ἐπορεξάμενος μεγαθύμου Τυδέος υἱὸς

ἄκρην οὔτασε χεῖρα μετάλμενος ὀξέϊ δουρὶ

ἀβληχρήν· εἶθαρ δὲ δόρυ χροὸς ἀντετόρησεν

ἀμβροσίου διὰ πέπλου, ὅν οἱ **Χάριτες** κάμον **αὐταί**,

πρυμνὸν ὕπερ θέναρος· ῥέε δ᾽ ἄμβροτον αἷμα θεοῖο,

340 ἰχώρ, οἷός πέρ τε ῥέει μακάρεσσι Θεοῖσιν·

οὐ γὰρ σῖτον ἔδουσ(ιν), οὐ πίνουσ(ιν) αἴθοπα οἶνον,

τοὔνεκ(α) ἀναίμονές εἰσι καὶ ἀθάνατοι καλέονται.

ἡ δὲ μέγα ἰάχουσα ἀπὸ ἕο κάββαλεν υἱόν·

καὶ τὸν μὲν μετὰ χερσὶν ἐρύσατο Φοῖβος Ἀπόλλων

345 κυανέῃ νεφέλῃ, μή τις Δαναῶν ταχυπώλων

χαλκὸν ἐνὶ στήθεσσι βαλὼν ἐκ θυμὸν ἕλοιτο·

τῇ δ᾽ ἐπὶ μακρὸν ἄϋσε βοὴν ἀγαθὸς Διομήδης·

"εἶκε, Διὸς θύγατερ, πολέμου καὶ δηϊοτῆτος·

ἦ οὐχ ἅλις ὅττι γυναῖκας ἀνάλκιδας ἠπεροπεύεις;

350 εἰ δὲ σύ γ᾽ ἐς πόλεμον πωλήσεαι, ἦ τέ **σ(ε)** ὀΐω

ῥιγήσειν πόλεμόν γε καὶ εἴ (κε) ἑτέρωθι πύθηαι."

ὡς ἔφα(το), ἡ δ᾽ ἀλύουσ(α) ἀπεβήσετο, τείρετο δ᾽ αἰνῶς·

WHAT HOMER ACTUALLY COMPOSED

Vocabulary

Ἀθηναίη, -ης, ἡ, Athena

Αἰνείας, -αο, ὁ, Aeneas

ἄντυξ, -υγος, ὁ, front rail of a chariot; shield rim

Ἀχαιοί, -ῶν, οἱ, Achaeans

Δηΐπυλος, -ου, ὁ, Deipylus

Διομήδης, -ους, ὁ, Diomedes

ἐμμεμαώς, -υῖα, eager

Ἐνυώ, -οῦς, ἡ, Enyo

ἐρύκω, —, ἔρυξα / ἠρύκακα, hold back, restrain

καλλίθριξ, καλλίτριχος, with beautiful hair

Καπανεύς, -ῆος, ὁ, Kapaneus

Κύπρις, -ιδος, ἡ, Cypris, i.e., Aphrodite

λανθάνω, λήσω, ἔλαθον, —, λέλασμαι, escape notice; *in mid.,* forget, + *gen.*

συνθεσίη, -ης, ἡ, *in pl.,* covenant, instructions

Τρῶοι, -ων, οἱ, Trojans

Τυδεΐδης, -ου, ὁ, Diomedes, son of Tydeus

ὑπεκφέρω, carry away from, + *gen.*

Notes

321   Sthenelus' restraint of his horses from the fighting is approximated skillfully by the word order; the verb, direct object, and three adjectives consume most of the line, creating the sense of straining to move ahead.

322   ONOMATOPOEIA is heard in **φλοίσβου.**

325–30   The six lines are nearly fully dactylic, with the final syllable of **φίλῳ** in the first line shortened by correption. The word ἵππων of line 328 provides the only spondaic interruption; one can almost hear the galloping hoof-beats.

329   The placement of **Τυδεΐδην** early in the line emphasizes the fact that Diomedes is Sthenelus' sole point of focus.

329–30   Notice the ENJAMBMENT. What other examples of this technique do you spot in the reading, and what is the effect?

333   Elsewhere in Homer Enyo is treated as the same goddess as Eris, a reminder of the backdrop of the action. Note and think about why Enyo receives an EPITHET, while Athena does not.

As It Was

ἡ μὲν ἐὸν φίλον υἱὸν ὑπεξέφερεν πολέμοιο·

οὐδ᾽ υἱὸς Καπανῆος ἐλήθετο συνθεσιάων

320 τάων ἃς ἐπέτελλε βοὴν ἀγαθὸς Διομήδης

ἀλλ᾽ ὅ γε τοὺς μὲν ἑοὺς ἠρύκακε μώνυχας ἵππους

νόσφιν ἀπὸ φλοίσβου, ἐξ ἄντυγος ἡνία τείνας,

Αἰνείαο δ᾽ ἐπαΐξας καλλίτριχας ἵππους

ἐξέλασε Τρώων μετ᾽ ἐϋκνήμιδας Ἀχαιούς.

325 δῶκε δὲ Δηϊπύλῳ, ἑτάρῳ φίλῳ, ὃν περὶ πάσης

τῖεν ὁμηλικίης, ὅτι οἱ φρεσὶν ἄρτια ἤδη,

νηυσὶν ἔπι γλαφυρῇσιν ἐλαυνέμεν· αὐτὰρ ὅ γ᾽ ἥρως

ὧν ἵππων ἐπιβὰς ἔλαβ᾽ ἡνία σιγαλόεντα,

αἶψα δὲ Τυδεΐδην μέθεπε κρατερώνυχας ἵππους

330 ἐμμεμαώς· ὁ δὲ Κύπριν ἐπῴχετο νηλέϊ χαλκῷ,

γιγνώσκων ὅ τ᾽ ἄναλκις ἔην θεός, οὐδὲ θεάων

τάων αἵ τ᾽ ἀνδρῶν πόλεμον κάτα κοιρανέουσιν,

οὔτ᾽ ἄρ᾽ Ἀθηναίη οὔτε πτολίπορθος Ἐνυώ.

Vocabulary

ἀλύω, be distressed

Ἀπόλλων, -ωνος, ὁ, Apollo

Δαναοί, -ῶν, οἱ, Danaans

Διομήδης, -ους, ὁ, Diomedes

ἐρύω, ἐρύω, εἴρυσα, ——, εἴρυσμαι, drag

Ζεύς, Διός, ὁ, Zeus

ἠπεροπεύω, deceive

θέναρ, -αρος, τό, wrist

καταβάλλω, ——, κατέβαλα, throw down, drop

πυνθάνομαι, πεύσομαι, ἐπυθόμην, ——, πέπυσμαι, learn by inquiry

Τυδεύς, -έος, ὁ, Tydeus

Φοῖβος, -ου, ὁ, Phoebus, *epithet of Apollo*

Χάριτες, -ων, αἱ, the Graces

Notes

334   Read this verse with attention to the meter. Observe how the dactyls reflect the action going on within the line.

336   The wounding of the goddess who is at the root of the conflict may serve to lighten the tone and provide relief from the overwhelming violence.

338   Notice the artful positioning of the preposition between adjective and noun; διά "pierces through" the ambrosial robe.

339–40   Note the repetition in ῥέε and ῥέει to reinforce the vivid image, a form of ANAPHORA.

341–42   The structure of these two lines features CHIASMUS followed by SYNCHESIS. What connection can you infer about such arrangement and the particular subject matter in these verses?

343   The scansion of this line is difficult. The alpha of μέγα must be scanned long because ἰάχουσα has lost an initial digamma. The omicron of ἀπό is scanned long because ἕο once began with two consonants, sigma and digamma (cf. Latin *suus*).

345–46   μὴ . . . ἕλοιτο: A REPETITION of Aphrodite's attempt to save Aeneas in the previous reading, lines 316–17.

347   τῇ: The pronoun takes the first position in the line, possibly anticipating the directness of Diomedes' manner of address to Aphrodite.

ἐπὶ . . . ἄϋσε: The adverbial μακρόν divides the verb by TMESIS.

349   The first two words of this line must be pronounced as a single syllable by synizesis.

350   The poet has Diomedes engage in wordplay in the juxtaposition of πόλεμον and πωλήσεαι. What effect is achieved in portraying a warrior capable of crafty speech in the presence of divinity?

As It Was (Continued)

ἀλλ᾽ ὅτε δή ῥ᾽ ἐκίχανε πολὺν καθ᾽ ὅμιλον ὀπάζων,

335   ἔνθ᾽ ἐπορεξάμενος μεγαθύμου Τυδέος υἱὸς

ἄκρην οὔτασε χεῖρα μετάλμενος ὀξέϊ δουρὶ

ἀβληχρήν· εἶθαρ δὲ δόρυ χροὸς ἀντετόρησεν

ἀμβροσίου διὰ πέπλου, ὅν οἱ Χάριτες κάμον αὐταί,

πρυμνὸν ὕπερ θέναρος· ῥέε δ᾽ ἄμβροτον αἷμα θεοῖο

340   ἰχώρ, οἷός πέρ τε ῥέει μακάρεσσι θεοῖσιν·

οὐ γὰρ σῖτον ἔδουσ᾽, οὐ πίνουσ᾽ αἴθοπα οἶνον,

τοὔνεκ᾽ ἀναίμονές εἰσι καὶ ἀθάνατοι καλέονται.

ἡ δὲ μέγα ἰάχουσα ἀπὸ ἔο κάββαλεν υἱόν·

καὶ τὸν μὲν μετὰ χερσὶν ἐρύσατο Φοῖβος Ἀπόλλων

345   κυανέῃ νεφέλῃ, μή τις Δαναῶν ταχυπώλων

χαλκὸν ἐνὶ στήθεσσι βαλὼν ἐκ θυμὸν ἕλοιτο·

τῇ δ᾽ ἐπὶ μακρὸν ἄϋσε βοὴν ἀγαθὸς Διομήδης·

"εἶκε, Διὸς θύγατερ, πολέμου καὶ δηϊοτῆτος·

ἦ οὐχ ἅλις ὅττι γυναῖκας ἀνάλκιδας ἠπεροπεύεις;

350   εἰ δὲ σύ γ᾽ ἐς πόλεμον πωλήσεαι, ἦ τέ σ᾽ ὀΐω

ῥιγήσειν πόλεμόν γε καὶ εἴ χ᾽ ἑτέρωθι πύθηαι."

ὣς ἔφαθ᾽, ἡ δ᾽ ἀλύουσ᾽ ἀπεβήσετο, τείρετο δ᾽ αἰνῶς·

AFTER READING WHAT HOMER COMPOSED

1. The scene is interesting for what it says about Diomedes. Are his actions in keeping with the warrior's code, given his primary foe and what he must do in order to pursue that foe?

2. Use this incident to discuss the *Iliad* as a poem largely concerned with family relationships.

3. What is your reaction to Diomedes' wounding of Aphrodite? Does this scene fit your expectations (a) of Diomedes as characterized in Reading 8, and (b) of deities as you generally perceive them?

4. What is your reaction to Diomedes' assertion that "Cypris . . . is a weak (ἄναλκις) divinity"?

READING 10

Andromache Begs Hector Not to Return to Battle

(Iliad 6.421–39)

BEFORE YOU READ WHAT HOMER COMPOSED

Introduction

Hector, the foremost fighter and hope of the Trojans, has broken from the fierce fighting to return within the walls. He meets his wife, Andromache, holding their infant son, and the two exchange words. When he tells her he must go back to the battle, the discussion becomes more urgent and poignant. Her long speech (6.407–39) expresses the desperate love and devotion she feels for him; at the same time, it demonstrates Homer's remarkable insight into humanity.

In his response subsequent to this reading, Hector reminds Andromache that he must be true to his duty and defend the city (6.440–65). The scene closes with a touching moment between Hector and his son (6.466–82).

Keep This Grammar in Mind — PARATAXIS

Homer's language tends to build the narrative through a series of coordinated clauses joined by conjunctions such as δέ, τε, and καί, often leaving the exact logical connection between clauses implied. Clauses may even display ASYNDETON, leaving no explicit connection at all between verbs. This linear or "side-by-side" arrangement is called **parataxis,** and is a significant characteristic of Homeric diction.

Keep This Grammar in Mind — HYPOTAXIS

Despite the prevalence of the paratactic arrangement, Homer makes use of subordinate clauses. The use of adverbial, adjectival, and noun clauses is **hypotaxis** ("subordinating arrangement").

Subordinate clauses are generally introduced by conjunctions, but the use of circumstantial participles is a quicker, more efficient way of introducing subordinate ideas. Participial phrases can be a valuable alternative to the use of subordinating conjunctions, and may enhance the impression of quickness in a narrative full of action.

Stopping for Some Practice — Hypotaxis and Parataxis

Andromache delivers the following sentences in this reading. Note whether the actions are joined with paratactic or hypotactic structures, and in the case of the latter, write the subordinating conjunctions and/or circumstantial participles that establish the subordinate ideas.

1. οἳ δέ μοι ἑπτὰ κασίγνητοι ἔσαν ἐν μεγάροισιν, / οἳ μὲν πάντες ἰῷ κίον ἤματι Ἄϊδος εἴσω.

   Structure(s) _____

   Subordinating word(s) _____

2. τὴν ἐπεὶ ἂρ δεῦρ᾽ ἤγαγ᾽ ἅμ᾽ ἄλλοισι κτεάτεσσιν, / ἂψ ὅ γε τὴν ἀπέλυσε λαβὼν ἀπερείσι᾽ ἄποινα.

   Structure(s) _____

   Subordinating word(s) _____

3. ἀλλ᾽ ἄγε νῦν ἐλέαιρε καὶ αὐτοῦ μίμν᾽ ἐπὶ πύργῳ.

   Structure(s) _____

   Subordinating word(s) _____

4. τρὶς γὰρ τῇ γ᾽ ἐλθόντες ἐπειρήσανθ᾽ οἱ ἄριστοι.

   Structure(s) _____

   Subordinating word(s) _____

HELPING YOU READ WHAT HOMER COMPOSED

Vocabulary

Ἀΐδης, -αο, ὁ, Hades, the underworld

ἀργεννός, -ή, -όν, white

Ἄρτεμις, -ιδος, ἡ, Artemis

Ἀχιλ(λ)εύς, -ῆος, ὁ, Achilles

ἄψ, again; back, backward

βοῦς, βοός, ὁ / ἡ, cattle

εἰλίπους, εἰλίποδος, with rolling gait

Ἕκτωρ, -ωρος, ὁ, Hector

ἦμαρ, -ατος, τό, day

θαλερός, -ή, -όν, blooming, fresh

ἰός, - ή, -όν, one, single

κατέπεφνον, *aor. only,* kill, slay

κίω, go, come

κτέαρ, -ατος, τό, possession

μέγαρον, -ου, τό, house, hall

παρακοίτης, -ου, ὁ, bed-mate

Πλάκος, -ου, ἡ, a mountain in Mysia

ὑληέσσος, -η, -ον, wooded

Notes

421   μοι: Andromache is the speaker.

ἑπτά: Most numbers are indeclinable adjs.

ἔσαν: < εἰμί, Attic = ἦσαν

421–22   οἵ: The rel. clause precedes the main clause, which is introduced by the demonst. pron. οἱ, "Those who were . . . . "

422   ἤματι: dat. of time at which

424   ἐπ᾽: "among"; note again the practice of surrounding the prep. with its objs.

ἀργεννῆς ὀίεσσι: also with ἐπ᾽

426   τήν: belongs to the clause that begins with ἐπεί; the word order is simply inverted (ANASTROPHE)

427   ἀπέλυσε λαβών: Aor. pples. indicate time prior to the main verb, even if that verb is also aor., "after he took the boundless ransom, he released her."

428   πατρός: Just as the obj. or a related adj. may precede a prep., so too a related gen.

429   ἀτάρ: = αὐτάρ

ἐσσί: 2ⁿᵈ sing. pres. indic. < εἰμί, Attic = εἶ

As You Read

425 What form is ἥ?

426–27 ἐπεὶ . . . λαβών: Notice the use of these two styles of hypotactic expression, the first introduced by a subordinating conjunction, the other a circumstantial participle. How does each contribute to the integrity and efficacy of the passage?

435 What is the first principal part of ἐλθόντες? What noun(s) does it modify?

438 What is the first principal part of εἰδώς? With what does it agree?

Summary

Hector must return to the fighting. Andromache begs him not to go. She reminds him that Achilles killed her entire family and Hector has thus become everything to her. She tells him to stay inside lest he make her a widow and his son an orphan.

Making Sense of It

You should be comfortable now with the elided forms of most common prepositions; their full forms will no longer appear in the pre-reading.

"οἳ δέ μοι ἑπτὰ κασίγνητοι ἔσαν ἐν μεγάροισιν,

οἱ μὲν πάντες ἰῷ κίον **ἤματι** Ἄϊδος εἴσω·

πάντας γὰρ κατέπεφνε **ποδάρκης δῖος Ἀχιλλεὺς**

βουσὶν ἐπ᾽ εἰλιπόδεσσι καὶ **ἀργεννῇς ὄϊεσσι.**

425   μητέρα δ᾽, ἣ βασίλευεν ὑπὸ Πλάκῳ ὑληέσσῃ,

τὴν ἐπεὶ ἂρ δεῦρ(ο) ἤγαγ(ε) ἅμ᾽ ἄλλοισι κτεάτεσσιν,

ἂψ ὅ γε τὴν ἀπέλυσε λαβὼν ἀπερείσι(α) ἄποινα,

πατρὸς δ᾽ ἐν μεγάροισι (αὐτὴν) (ἔ)βαλ(ε) Ἄρτεμις ἰοχέαιρα.

Ἕκτορ, ἀτὰρ σύ μοί ἐσσι πατὴρ καὶ πότνια μήτηρ

430   ἠδὲ κασίγνητος, σὺ δέ μοι **θαλερὸς παρακοίτης·**

Vocabulary

ἀγακλυτός, -όν, very famous, glorious

Αἴας, -αντος, ὁ, Ajax

ἀμβατός, -όν, capable of being scaled

ἀνώγω, ἀνώξω, ἤνωξα, ἄνωγα, order, command

Ἀτρεΐδης, -αο, ὁ, son of Atreus

ἐλεαίρω, pity

ἐννέπω, ἐνίψω, ἔνισπον, say, tell

ἐποτρύνω, ——, ἐπώτρυνα, stir to action, incite, urge

ἐρινεός, -οῦ, ὁ, wild fig tree

Ἰδομενεύς, -ῆος, ὁ, Idomeneus

μίμνω, μενέω, ἔμεινα, remain

πειράω, πειρήσω, ἐπειρησάμην, ——, πεπείρημαι, try, attempt, make trial of

πύργος, -ου, ὁ, tower

Τυδεύς, -έος, ὁ, Tydeus

χήρη, -ης, ἡ, widow

Notes

431 ἄγε: idiomatically, "Come now . . ."
        αὐτοῦ: "here"

432 μὴ . . . θήῃς: aor. subjnc. < τίθημι, used as a polite imperat., "Please don't make . . . "

433 στῆσον: aor. imperat. < ἵστημι, "station"

434 ἔπλετο: aor. < πέλομαι, translate as pres.

435 τῇ: "in that place"

436 Αἴαντε: "The two Ajaxes." The poet uses a dual ending here, but refers to the two Atreidai in the next line as pl.

437 Τυδέος . . . υἱόν: i.e., Diomedes

438 τίς: accented because of following enclitic
        θεοπροπίων: gen. pl. after ἐΰ εἰδώς, "knowledgeable concerning . . . "
        εἰδώς: pple. < οἶδα

Making Sense of It (Continued)

ἀλλ᾽ ἄγε νῦν ἐλέαιρε καὶ αὐτοῦ μίμν(ε) ἐπὶ (τῷ) πύργῳ,

μὴ **παῖδ(α) ὀρφανικὸν** θήῃς **χήρην** τε **γυναῖκα·**

λαὸν δὲ στῆσον παρ᾽ ἐρινεόν, ἔνθα μάλιστα

ἀμβατός ἐστι **πόλις** καὶ ἐπίδρομον ἔπλετο (τὸ) τεῖχος.

435   τρὶς γὰρ τῇ γ᾽ **ἐλθόντες** ἐπειρήσαντ(ο) **οἱ ἄριστοι**

ἀμφ᾽ **Αἴαντε δύω** καὶ ἀγακλυτὸν Ἰδομενῆα

ἠδ(ὲ) ἀμφ᾽ (τοὺς) Ἀτρεΐδας καὶ Τυδέυς (τὸν) ἄλκιμον υἱόν·

ἤ πού τίς σφιν ἔνισπε θεοπροπίων ἐῢ εἰδώς,

ἤ νυ καὶ αὐτῶν θυμὸς ἐποτρύνει καὶ ἀνώγει."

WHAT HOMER ACTUALLY COMPOSED

Vocabulary

ἀγακλυτός, -όν, very famous, glorious

Αἴας, -αντος, ὁ, Ajax

Ἀΐδης, -αο, ὁ, Hades, the underworld

ἀμβατός, -όν, capable of being scaled

ἀνώγω, ἀνώξω, ἤνωξα, ἄνωγα, order, command

ἀργεννός, -ή, -όν, white

Ἄρτεμις, -ιδος, ἡ, Artemis

Ἀτρεΐδης, -αο, ὁ, son of Atreus

Ἀχιλ(λ)εύς, -ῆος, ὁ, Achilles

ἄψ, again; back, backward

βοῦς, βοός, ὁ / ἡ, cattle

εἰλίπους, εἰλίποδος, with rolling gait

Ἕκτωρ, -ωρος, ὁ, Hector

ἐλεαίρω, pity

ἐννέπω, ἐνίψω, ἔνισπον, say, tell

ἐποτρύνω, —, ἐπώτρυνα, stir to action, incite, urge

ἐρινεός, -οῦ, ὁ, wild fig tree

ἦμαρ, -ατος, τό, day

θαλερός, -ή, -όν, blooming, fresh

Ἰδομενεύς, -ῆος, ὁ, Idomeneus

ἰός, - ή, -όν, one, single

κατέπεφνον, aor. only, kill, slay

κίω, go, come

κτέαρ, -ατος, τό, possession

μέγαρον, -ου, τό, house, hall

μίμνω, μενέω, ἔμεινα, remain

παρακοίτης, -ου, ὁ, bed-mate

πειράω, πειρήσω, ἐπειρησάμην, —, πεπείρημαι, try, attempt, make trial of

Πλάκος, -ου, ἡ, a mountain in Mysia

πύργος, -ου, ὁ, tower

Τυδεύς, -έος, ὁ, Tydeus

ὑλήεσσος, -η, -ον, wooded

χήρη, -ης, ἡ, widow

Notes

422 ἰῷ κίον ἤματι: The line falls into three units, with this key phrase carefully positioned in the center.

423 κατέπεφνε: The verb is set immediately before the caesura (see p. xviii) with Achilles' name and formulaic EPITHET filling out the second half of the line. Careful study of word and phrase placement will deepen one's enjoyment of the poem.

427 ἀπερείσι᾿ ἄποινα: The acceptance or rejection of ransom is a strong theme in the *Iliad*. Recall that it was Agamemnon's refusal to accept the ransom for Chryses that began his argument with Achilles, a decision that he later had to reverse. At the end of the poem, Achilles will accept ransom from Priam in person in exchange for Hector's corpse. Thus the idea of accepting/rejecting ransom brackets the poem.

428 Ἄρτεμις ἰοχέαιρα: Artemis is a goddess of the hunt, and Apollo's sister.

429 σύ μοι: Note the artful placement of the pronouns.

431 ἄγε . . . ἐλέαιρε: ASYNDETON is standard following this use of ἄγε.

432 παῖδ᾿ ὀρφανικὸν . . . χήρην τε γυναῖκα: Note the CHIASMUS created by the inversion of each noun relative to its adjective. The number of syllables on either side of the verb is the same, giving the line a remarkable balance. As the climactic line of one of the most powerful scenes in the poem, it reflects careful craftsmanship.

433 λαὸν δὲ στῆσον: It is striking that Andromache should offer strategic advice to her husband. Just as in the *Odyssey* Penelope's cleverness with her weaving proves her a match for Odysseus, so here Andromache shows that she is a worthy mate for Hector.

As It Was

"οἳ δέ μοι ἑπτὰ κασίγνητοι ἔσαν ἐν μεγάροισιν,

οἳ μὲν πάντες ἰῷ κίον ἤματι Ἄϊδος εἴσω·

πάντας γὰρ κατέπεφνε ποδάρκης δῖος Ἀχιλλεὺς

βουσὶν ἐπ᾽ εἰλιπόδεσσι καὶ ἀργεννῇς ὄιεσσι.

425 μητέρα δ᾽, ἣ βασίλευεν ὑπὸ Πλάκῳ ὑληέσσῃ,

τὴν ἐπεὶ ἀρ δεῦρ᾽ ἤγαγ᾽ ἅμ᾽ ἄλλοισι κτεάτεσσιν,

ἂψ ὅ γε τὴν ἀπέλυσε λαβὼν ἀπερείσι᾽ ἄποινα,

πατρὸς δ᾽ ἐν μεγάροισι βάλ᾽ Ἄρτεμις ἰοχέαιρα.

Ἕκτορ, ἀτὰρ σύ μοί ἐσσι πατὴρ καὶ πότνια μήτηρ

430 ἠδὲ κασίγνητος, σὺ δέ μοι θαλερὸς παρακοίτης·

ἀλλ᾽ ἄγε νῦν ἐλέαιρε καὶ αὐτοῦ μίμν᾽ ἐπὶ πύργῳ,

μὴ παῖδ᾽ ὀρφανικὸν θήῃς χήρην τε γυναῖκα·

λαὸν δὲ στῆσον πάρ᾽ ἐρινεόν, ἔνθα μάλιστα

ἀμβατός ἐστι πόλις καὶ ἐπίδρομον ἔπλετο τεῖχος.

435 τρὶς γὰρ τῇ γ᾽ ἐλθόντες ἐπειρήσανθ᾽ οἱ ἄριστοι

ἀμφ᾽ Αἴαντε δύω καὶ ἀγακλυτὸν Ἰδομενῆα

ἠδ᾽ ἀμφ᾽ Ἀτρεΐδας καὶ Τυδέος ἄλκιμον υἱόν·

ἤ πού τίς σφιν ἔνισπε θεοπροπίων ἐῢ εἰδώς,

ἤ νυ καὶ αὐτῶν θυμὸς ἐποτρύνει καὶ ἀνώγει."

AFTER READING WHAT HOMER COMPOSED

1. If you were in Hector's position, how would you respond to Andromache's appeal?

2. How do you account for the sympathetic portrayal of Hector and Andromache to a Greek audience?

3. We learn a great deal about Achilles from seeing him through the eyes of other characters, especially women. How does Andromache's story of her family affect your understanding of Achilles? Why should Homer have chosen Andromache to convey this information?

READING 11

Homer Surveys the Battlefield

(*Iliad* 16.306–29)

BEFORE YOU READ WHAT HOMER COMPOSED

Introduction

Homer's poetry is remarkable for its sense of rhythm. As the war rages on, the battle scenes become increasingly violent and descriptions of the bloodshed become increasingly graphic. The level of ferocity builds to a point that is hardly bearable until climactic events pour out one after another. The following readings survey the battlefield prior to the death of Patroclus, Achilles' close companion.

Keep This Grammar in Mind — USES OF ὡς

The word ὡς has a variety of meanings. Three basic ideas are commonly used:

- ὥς or ὧς (with accent) = οὕτως, "thus, in this way";
- ὡς (with no accent) introduces a simile, "like" or "as";
- and ὡς is also a conjunction introducing purpose, etc., "that" or "how."

Keep This Grammar in Mind — PERSONAL AGENT

In a passive construction the subject is the receiver of the action, while the action is done by an **agent.** In the sentence, "The soldier is stopped by the general," the soldier is the subject, but unlike in an active construction, he is not *doing* anything; the agent actually performing the action is the general. That same situation could be expressed actively by the sentence, "The general stops the soldier."

While Attic Greek tends to show personal agency by a *genitive* noun or pronoun following ὑπό, Homer often uses a *dative* noun or pronoun, with no preposition:

ὣς τὼ μὲν **δοιοῖσι κασιγνήτοισι** δαμέντε βήτην εἰς Ἔρεβος . . .

Stopping for Some Practice — ὡς

The first three statements below you will recognize from earlier readings. Review these, noting in particular the use of ὡς. The last sentence you will encounter in this reading. Study it (don't forget about duals!), and try to anticipate the meaning of ὡς.

1. ὡς ἔμ᾽ ἀφαιρεῖται Χρυσηΐδα Φοῖβος Ἀπόλλων,
    τὴν μὲν ἐγὼ σὺν νηΐ τ᾽ ἐμῇ καὶ ἐμοῖς ἑτάροισι
    πέμψω.

    Meaning _____

2. ὣς δ᾽ αὔτως Μενέλαος ἀρήϊος ἔντε᾽ ἔδυνεν.

    Meaning _____

3. βαῖνε λέων ὣς ἀλκὶ πεποιθώς
    πρόσθε δέ οἱ δόρυ τ᾽ ἔσχε καὶ ἀσπίδα πάντοσ᾽ ἐΐσην.

    Meaning _____

4. ὣς τὼ μὲν δοιοῖσι κασιγνήτοιοι δαμέντε βήτην εἰς Ἔρεβος.

    Meaning _____

Helping You Read What Homer Composed

Vocabulary

ἄλκιμος, -η, -ον, strong

Ἄμφικλος, -ου, ὁ, Amphiclus

Ἀρηΐλυκος, -ου, ὁ, Areilycus

ἀρήϊος, -η, -ον, warlike

γυμνόω, —, —, —, —, ἐγυμνώθην, strip; *in pass.*, to be defenseless

διασχίζω, —, διέσχισα, —, —, διεσχίσθην, sever, tear

δοκεύω, watch closely

ἐφορμάω, —, ἐφώρμησα, —, —, ἐφωρμήθην, incite; *mid. / pass.*, rush upon

θόας, -αντος, ὁ, Thoas

καταπίπτω, —, κάππεσον, fall down

κεδάννυμι, —, ἐκέδασσα, —, —, ἐκεδάσθην, scatter, disperse

Μενέλαος, -ου, ὁ, Menelaus

Μενοίτιος, -ου, ὁ, Menoetius

μηρός, -οῦ, ὁ, thigh

μυών, -ῶνος, ὁ, muscle

ὀξυόεις, -εσσα, -εν, pointed

ὀρέγω, ὀρέξω, ὤρεξα, —, ὀρώρεχαμαι, hold out, stretch

οὐτάω, —, οὔτά, —, —, wound

παχύς, -εῖα, -ύ, thick, stout

πρηνής, -ές, prone, falling headlong

πρυμνός, -ή, -όν, hindmost part; base

σκότος, -ου, ὁ, darkness

στέρνον, -ου, τό, chest

Φυλεΐδης, -εος, ὁ, Megas, son of Phyleus

Notes

306   κεδασθείσης ὑσμίνης: gen. absolute, "when the battle-line was broken"; Homer now focuses on individuals in the melee

307   ἡγεμόνων: partit. gen., "among the leaders"

   Μενοιτίου . . . υἱός: i.e., Patroclus

308   βάλε: augment omitted, as often; cf. ῥῆξεν, line 310

309   χαλκόν: "spear head," by METONYMY

311   κάππεσ᾿: < καταπίπτω

312   στέρνον: acc. of respect, frequent with body parts

314   ἔφθη: < φθάνω

   ὀρεξάμενος: < ὀρέγω, here meaning not only to "reach," but also to "hit"

   πρυμνὸν σκέλος: i.e., near the gluteus maximus

   πάχιστος: superl. adj. < παχύς

316   ὄσσε: dual acc. of respect, "covered him in respect to his eyes," but essentially, "covered his eyes"

Summary

Patroclus leads the Greeks against the Trojans. Heroes fall from various wounds as each man picks out an opponent. Homer spares nothing of the brutality of hand-to-hand combat.

From this point on, the visual aids in the altered text will be diminished. You must rely on what you have learned about how Homer writes, what words go together, and what words or letters are elided. The final two readings will not include altered text.

Making Sense of It

ἔνθα δ᾽ ἀνὴρ ἕλεν ἄνδρα κεδασθείσης ὑσμίνης

ἡγεμόνων. πρῶτος δὲ Μενοιτίου ἄλκιμος υἱὸς

αὐτίκ᾽ ἄρα **στρεφθέντος Ἀρηϊλύκου** βάλε μηρὸν

ἔγχεϊ ὀξυόεντι, διαπρὸ δὲ χαλκὸν ἔλασσε·

310   ῥῆξεν δ᾽ ὀστέον ἔγχος, ὁ δὲ πρηνὴς ἐπὶ γαίη

κάππεσ᾽· ἀτὰρ Μενέλαος ἀρήϊος οὖτα Θόαντα

στέρνον γυμνωθέντα παρ᾽ ἀσπίδα, λῦσε δὲ γυῖα.

Φυλεΐδης δ᾽ **Ἄμφικλον ἐφορμηθέντα** δοκεύσας

ἔφθη ὀρεξάμενος πρυμνὸν σκέλος, ἔνθα πάχιστος

315   μυῶν ἀνθρώπου πέλεται· περὶ δ᾽ ἔγχεος αἰχμῇ

νεῦρα διεσχίσθη· τὸν δὲ σκότος ὄσσε κάλυψε.

Vocabulary

αἱρέω, αἱρήσω, εἷλον, take hold of, seize; *in mid.*, choose

ἀκωκή, -ῆς, ἡ, spear point

ἀμαιμάκετος, -η, -ον, huge

Ἀμισώδαρος, -ου, ὁ, Amisodarus

Ἀντίλοχος, -ου, Antilochus

ἀπαράσσω, —, ἀπήραξα, smash

Ἀτύμνιος, -ου, Atymnius

ἀφαμαρτάνω, —, ἀφάρματον / ἀπήμβροτον, miss one's aim

ἄχρις, utterly, completely

δαμάζω, tame, overcome

δρύπτω, —, ἐδρύψα, —, —, ἐδρύφθη, strip off

ἐλαύνω, ἐλά(σ)(σ)ω, ἤλασ(σ)α, —, ἐλήλαμαι, drive

ἐπορούω, —, ἐπόρουσα, attack, + *dat.*

Ἔρεβος, -ου, ὁ, Erebus

Θρασυμήδης, -εος, ὁ, Thrasymedes

Μάρις, -ιδος, ὁ, Maris

νέκυς -υος, ὁ, corpse

Νεστορίδης, -εος, son of Nestor

ὀστέον, -ου, τό, bone

ῥήγνυμι, ῥήξω, ἔρρηξα, break

Σαρπηδών, -όνος, ὁ, Sarpedon

Χίμαιρα, -ας, ἡ, the Chimaera

Notes

317 **Νεστορίδαι:** "the two sons of Nestor," Antilochus and Thrasymedes; their actions are split into μέν and (line 321) δέ clauses as they kill two Trojan brothers, Atumnius and Maris.

318 **διήλασε:** the prefix calls for the gen., "through the hollow under the ribs"

321 **στάς:** aor. pple. < ἵστημι

322 **οὐτάσαι:** aor. infin. following πρίν, with Maris as the subj.

323 **ὦμον:** obj. of ὀρεξάμενος; cf. line 314

πρυμνὸν ... βραχίονα: "upper arm"

324 **ἀπὸ ... ἄραξε:** In Homer verbal prefixes often reflect their origin as discrete advs. (see TMESIS); read as though from ἀπαράσσω.

326 **τὼ ... δαμέντε:** dual aor. pass. pple.

κασιγνήτοισι: agents regularly appear in the dat.

327 **βήτην:** dual aor. < βαίνω

εἰς Ἔρεβος: "to the underworld"

329 **θρέψεν:** aor. < τρέφω

πολέσιν: < πολύς

κακόν: in apposition with the Chimaera

Making Sense of It (Continued)

Νεστορίδαι δ᾽ ὁ μὲν οὖτασ᾽ Ἀτύμνιον ὀξέϊ δουρὶ

Ἀντίλοχος, λαπάρης δὲ διήλασε χάλκεον ἔγχος·

ἤριπε δὲ προπάροιθε. Μάρις δ᾽ αὐτοσχεδὰ δουρὶ

320   Ἀντιλόχῳ ἐπόρουσε κασιγνήτοιο χολωθείς,

στὰς πρόσθεν νέκυος· τοῦ δ᾽ ἀντίθεος Θρασυμήδης

ἔφθη ὀρεξάμενος πρὶν οὐτάσαι, οὐδ᾽ ἀφάμαρτεν,

ὦμον ἄφαρ· **πρυμνὸν** δὲ **βραχίονα** δουρὸς ἀκωκὴ

δρύψ᾽ ἀπὸ μυώνων, ἀπὸ δ᾽ ὀστέον ἄχρις ἄραξε·

325   δούπησεν δὲ πεσών, κατὰ δὲ σκότος ὄσσε κάλυψεν.

ὣς τὼ μὲν δοιοῖσι κασιγνήτοισι δαμέντε

βήτην εἰς Ἔρεβος, Σαρπηδόνος ἐσθλοὶ ἑταῖροι,

υἷες ἀκοντισταὶ Ἀμισωδάρου, ὅς ῥα Χίμαιραν

θρέψεν ἀμαιμακέτην, πολέσιν κακὸν ἀνθρώποισιν.

WHAT HOMER ACTUALLY COMPOSED

Vocabulary

ἄλκιμος, -η, -ον, strong

Ἄμφικλος, -ου, ὁ, Amphiclus

Ἀρηΐλυκος, -ου, ὁ, Areilycus

ἀρήϊος, -η, -ον, warlike

γυμνόω, —, —, —, —, ἐγυμνώθην, strip; *in pass.*, to be defenseless

διασχίζω, —, διέσχισα, —, —, διεσχίσθην, sever, tear

δοκεύω, watch closely

ἐφορμάω, —, ἐφώρμησα, —, —, ἐφωρμήθην, incite; *mid. / pass.*, rush upon

θόας, -αντος, ὁ, Thoas

καταπίπτω, —, κάππεσον, fall down

κεδάννυμι, —, ἐκέδασσα, —, —, ἐκεδάσθην, scatter, disperse

Μενέλαος, -ου, ὁ, Menelaus

Μενοίτιος, -ου, ὁ, Menoetius

μηρός, -οῦ, ὁ, thigh

μυών, -ῶνος, ὁ, muscle

ὀξυόεις, -εσσα, -εν, pointed

ὀρέγω, ὀρέξω, ὤρεξα, —, ὀρωρέχαμαι, hold out, stretch

οὐτάω, —, οὐτά, —, —, wound

παχύς, -εῖα, -ύ, thick, stout

πρηνής, -ές, prone, falling headlong

πρυμνός, -ή, -όν, hindmost part; base

σκότος, -ου, ὁ, darkness

στέρνον, -ου, τό, chest

Φυλεΐδης, -εος, ὁ, Megas, son of Phyleus

Notes

307   ἡγεμόνων: The ENJAMBMENT pulls the reader forward and is particularly effective in conveying the speed at which events occur in battle.

πρῶτος: The force is adverbial in English. The ordinal adjective was commonly used in this way.

310–11   Note the effect of the ENJAMBMENT; as κάππεσ' spills into the next line anticipation is created.

312   στέρνον γυμνωθέντα: Presumably this indicates an unprotected area that allows for the free movement of the shield arm.

λῦσε δὲ γυῖα: a frequent euphemism for death in battle, "he loosened his limbs." What euphemisms do we use for death?

314   πρυμνὸν σκέλος: If the femoral artery were pierced, death from blood loss would follow quickly.

315   περὶ δ' ἔγχεος αἰχμῇ: The object of the preposition is delayed by the preceding genitive.

316   σκότος ὄσσε κάλυψε: This is another common euphemism (see line 325), "darkness covered his (two) eyes."

As It Was

ἔνθα δ᾿ ἀνὴρ ἕλεν ἄνδρα κεδασθείσης ὑσμίνης
ἡγεμόνων. πρῶτος δὲ Μενοιτίου ἄλκιμος υἱὸς
αὐτίκ᾿ ἄρα στρεφθέντος Ἀρηϊλύκου βάλε μηρὸν
ἔγχεϊ ὀξυόεντι, διαπρὸ δὲ χαλκὸν ἔλασσε·
310   ῥῆξεν δ᾿ ὀστέον ἔγχος, ὁ δὲ πρηνὴς ἐπὶ γαίη
κάππεσ᾿· ἀτὰρ Μενέλαος ἀρήϊος οὖτα Θόαντα
στέρνον γυμνωθέντα παρ᾿ ἀσπίδα, λῦσε δὲ γυῖα.
Φυλεΐδης δ᾿ Ἄμφικλον ἐφορμηθέντα δοκεύσας
ἔφθη ὀρεξάμενος πρυμνὸν σκέλος, ἔνθα πάχιστος
315   μυῶν ἀνθρώπου πέλεται· περὶ δ᾿ ἔγχεος αἰχμῇ
νεῦρα διεσχίσθη· τὸν δὲ σκότος ὄσσε κάλυψε.

Vocabulary

αἱρέω, αἱρήσω, εἷλον, take hold of, seize; *in mid.*, choose

ἀκωκή, -ῆς, ἡ, spear point

ἀμαιμάκετος, -η, -ον, huge

Ἀμισώδαρος, -ου, ὁ, Amisodarus

Ἀντίλοχος, -ου, Antilochus

ἀπαράσσω, —, ἀπήραξα, smash

Ἀτύμνιος, -ου, Atymnius

ἀφαμαρτάνω, —, ἀφάρματον / ἀπήμβροτον, miss one's aim

ἄχρις, utterly, completely

δαμάζω, tame, overcome

δρύπτω, —, ἐδρύψα, —, —, ἐδρύφθη, strip off

ἐλαύνω, ἐλά(σ)(σ)ω, ἤλασ(σ)α, —, ἐλήλαμαι, drive

ἐπορούω, —, ἐπόρουσα, attack, + *dat.*

Ἔρεβος, -ου, ὁ, Erebus

Θρασυμήδης, -εος, ὁ, Thrasymedes

Μάρις, -ιδος, ὁ, Maris

νέκυς -υος, ὁ, corpse

Νεστορίδης, -εος, son of Nestor

ὀστέον, -ου, τό, bone

ῥήγνυμι, ῥήξω, ἔρρηξα, break

Σαρπηδών, -όνος, ὁ, Sarpedon

Χίμαιρα, -ας, ἡ, the Chimaera

Notes

326–27 τὼ ... δαμέντε ... βήτην: The duals are immediately followed by plurals for the same subjects.

318 Ἀντίλοχος: Antilochus features prominently in the funeral games for Patroclus near the end of the *Iliad*. In a lost epic, the *Aithiopis,* it is the death of Antilochus at the hands of the hero Memnon that spurs Achilles into his final battle, in which he first avenges Antilochus, and is then himself brought down by the bow of Paris.

321 στὰς πρόσθεν νέκυος: The defense of a comrade's corpse to prevent the enemy from despoiling the armor as a prize is a frequently expanded formulaic element in Homeric battle scenes.

325 What is the effect of the harsh sounds in the last part of this line? Note the metrics in the opening of this line. What effect do those long syllables have in imagining this scene?

328 Ἀμισωδάρου: The poet takes care to situate his story in relation to previous generations of heroes. Why should the poet think it important to tell his audience that Amisodarus nourished the Chimaera?

As It Was (Continued)

Νεστορίδαι δ᾽ ὁ μὲν οὔτασ᾽ Ἀτύμνιον ὀξέϊ δουρὶ

Ἀντίλοχος, λαπάρης δὲ διήλασε χάλκεον ἔγχος·

ἤριπε δὲ προπάροιθε. Μάρις δ᾽ αὐτοσχεδὰ δουρὶ

320   Ἀντιλόχῳ ἐπόρουσε κασιγνήτοιο χολωθείς,

στὰς πρόσθεν νέκυος· τοῦ δ᾽ ἀντίθεος Θρασυμήδης

ἔφθη ὀρεξάμενος πρὶν οὐτάσαι, οὐδ᾽ ἀφάμαρτεν,

ὦμον ἄφαρ· πρυμνὸν δὲ βραχίονα δουρὸς ἀκωκὴ

δρύψ᾽ ἀπὸ μυώνων, ἀπὸ δ᾽ ὀστέον ἄχρις ἄραξε·

325   δούπησεν δὲ πεσών, κατὰ δὲ σκότος ὄσσε κάλυψεν.

ὣς τὼ μὲν δοιοῖσι κασιγνήτοιοι δαμέντε

βήτην εἰς Ἔρεβος, Σαρπηδόνος ἐσθλοὶ ἑταῖροι,

υἷες ἀκοντισταὶ Ἀμισωδάρου, ὅς ῥα Χίμαιραν

θρέψεν ἀμαιμακέτην, πολέσιν κακὸν ἀνθρώποισιν.

AFTER READING WHAT HOMER COMPOSED

1. The battlefield descriptions above may be seen as underscoring the brutality of war. Alternatively, such graphic scenes may simply reflect a matter-of-fact view of death. What do you think is the effect of the detailed portrayal of violence in war?

2. How does Homer maintain interest in the battlefield narrative?

3. Many heroes who die in this reading appear nowhere else in the poem, but Homer still gives them names. What is the effect of that?

READING 12

Greek Warriors Best the Trojans in a Fierce Battle

(*Iliad* 16.330–57)

Introduction

The brutality of war is extremely immediate in Homer's poetry. These images can shed light on the traumatic experience of modern warfare. Jonathan Shay, a psychiatrist engaged with veterans of the war in Vietnam, has explored the connections between the experiences of modern soldiers and the psychological insights of the *Iliad* (1994) and *Odyssey* (2002). His work has shown that the psychological experience of warfare was very much the same for Achilles, Odysseus, and their comrades as for modern soldiers.

Keep This Grammar in Mind — The Verb ἵημι

The common verb ἵημι means "to let go, send forth (eagerly)." In the middle voice, the meaning shifts toward "being eager."

ἵημι, ἥσω, ἧκα, εἷκα, εἷμαι, εἷθην [the latter appears only in compounds]

When compounded with prepositions, ἵημι retains its basic meaning and adds the extra dimension provided by the preposition. For example, "to let down" the sails of a ship is a compound of ἵημι with κατά.

This verb is troublesome because its forms appear similar to those of εἰμί and εἶμι. Keep in mind that only ἵημι has a rough breathing.

Stopping for Some Practice — ἵημι

At the very beginning of the *Iliad*, you encountered the verb ἵημι, in a prefixed form of the sort mentioned above. Review the first example below. You will read the others in later selections. Look carefully for each appearance of ἵημι, and identify its form, before translating.

1. τίς τ᾽ ἄρ σφωε θεῶν ἔριδι ξυνέηκε μάχεσθαι;
    [Reading 2 notes line 8, p. 10]

    Voice and Tense _____

    Translation _____

2. ὡς ἔρις ἔκ τε θεῶν ἔκ τ᾽ ἀνθρώπων ἀπόλοιτο,
    καὶ χόλος, ὅς τ᾽ ἐφέηκε πολύφρονά περ χαλεπῆναι . . .
    [Reading 14 notes lines 107–108, p. 102]

    Voice and Tense _____

    Translation _____

3.   καλαὶ δὲ περισσείοντο ἔθειραι
    χρύσεαι, ἃς Ἥφαιστος ἵει λόφον ἀμφὶ θαμειάς.
    [Reading 15 notes lines 315–16, p. 104]

    Voice and Tense _____

    Translation _____

HELPING YOU READ WHAT HOMER COMPOSED

Vocabulary

Αἴας, -αντος, ὁ, Ajax

Ἀκάμας, -αντος, ὁ, Acamas

βλάπτω, —, ἔβλαψα, —, —, ἐβλάβην, harm; catch, impede

δύω / δύνω, δύσω, ἔδυσα / ἔδυν, δέδυκα, sink

ἐρείπω, —, ἤριπα, throw down; *in aor.,* fall

θείνω, —, ἔθεινα, strike

ἱππόκομος, -η, -ον, with horse-hair crest

καρπάλιμος, -ον, swift

καυλός, -οῦ, ὁ, spear shaft; sword hilt

κιχάνω, κιχήσομαι, ἔκιχον, meet, reach

Κλεόβουλος, -ου, ὁ, Cleobulus

κλόνος, -ου, ὁ, confusion, panic of warfare

κωπήεις, -εσσα, -εν, hilted

Λύκων, -ονος, ὁ, Lycon

μέλεος, -η, -ον, vain, useless, empty

Μηριόνης, -εος, ὁ, Meriones

νύσσω, —, ἔνυξα, wound, pierce; thrust

Ὀϊλιάδης, -εος, ὁ, Ajax, son of Oeleus

ὄσσε, τώ, *dual,* eyes

οὖας, -ατος, τό, ear

ὄχεα, -ων, τά, *pl.,* chariot

παραείρω, —, —, —, —, παρηέρθην, detach; *in pass.,* hang down on one side

Πηνέλεως, ὁ, Peneleus

πλήσσω, —, ἔπληξα, πέπληγα, strike

πορφύρεος, -η, -ον, purple; gushing

ῥαίω, ῥαίσομαι, ἔραισα, —, —, ἐρραίσθην, shatter, break in pieces

συντρέχω, —, συνέδραμον, rush together

ὑποθερμαίνω, —, —, —, —, ὑπεθερμάνθην, *aor. pass.,* become heated

ὑπολύω, loose from under, undo

φάλος, -ου, ὁ, helmet device bearing a plume

Notes

331 βλαφθέντα: aor. pass. pple. < βλάπτω

κατὰ κλόνον: "in the confusion of battle"

334 ἔλλαβε: aor. < λαμβάνω; the double consonant reflects metrical necessity

335 ἔγχεσι: dat. pl. < ἔγχος

336 ἤμβροτον: aor. < ἁμαρτάνω

μέλεον: neut. acc. adj. used as adv.

337 τώ: dual pron. with pl. verb

338 ἤλασεν: aor. < ἐλαύνω

340 ἔσχεθε: a rare, poetic aor. < ἔχω

341 δέρμα: subj., "only the skin held (it)"

342 κιχείς: aor. pple. < κιχάνω

343 ἐπιβησόμενον: fut. pple. < ἐπιβαίνω + gen., "about to mount . . . "; presumably in order to flee

κατά: shows area affected with verbs of striking, "in the right shoulder"

Summary

Homer follows four pairs of heroes as they engage in close combat. This selection is an excerpt from a scene of five hundred lines gruesomely describing such encounters.

Making Sense of It

330 **Αἴας** δὲ Κλεόβουλον Ὀϊλιάδης **ἐπορούσας**

ζωὸν ἕλε, βλαφθέντα κατὰ κλόνον· ἀλλά οἱ αὖθι

λῦσε μένος, πλήξας **ξίφει** αὐχένα **κωπήεντι.**

πᾶν δ᾽ ὑπεθερμάνθη ξίφος αἵματι· τὸν δὲ κατ᾽ ὄσσε

ἔλλαβε πορφύρεος θάνατος καὶ **μοῖρα κραταιή.**

335 Πηνέλεως δὲ Λύκων τε συνέδραμον· ἔγχεσι μὲν γὰρ

ἤμβροτον ἀλλήλων, μέλεον δ᾽ ἠκόντισαν ἄμφω·

τὼ δ᾽ αὖτις ξιφέεσσι συνέδραμον. ἔνθα Λύκων **μὲν**

ἱπποκόμου κόρυθος φάλον ἤλασεν, ἀμφὶ **δὲ** *καυλὸν*

φάσγανον ἐρραίσθη· ὁ δ᾽ ὑπ᾽ οὔατος αὐχένα θεῖνε

340 Πηνέλεως, πᾶν δ᾽ εἴσω ἔδυ ξίφος, ἔσχεθε δ᾽ οἶον

δέρμα, παρηέρθη δὲ κάρη, ὑπέλυντο δὲ γυῖα.

Μηριόνης δ᾽ Ἀκάμαντα κιχεὶς ποσὶ καρπαλίμοισι

νύξ(ε) ἵππων ἐπιβησόμενον κατὰ δεξιὸν ὦμον·

ἤριπε δ᾽ ἐξ ὀχέων, κατὰ δ᾽ ὀφθαλμῶν κέχυτ(ο) ἀχλύς.

Vocabulary

ἄναλκις, incapable of defense; unsuited for battle

ἀντικρύ, straight through

ἀφραδίη, -ης, ἡ, senselessness, recklessness

Δαναοί, -ῶν, οἱ, Danaans

διατμήγω, —, διέτμηξα / διέτμαγον, —, —, διετμάγην, divide in two, sever

δυσκέλαδος, -ον, full of cries

ἐκπεράω, —, ἐξεπέρησα, pass through

ἐπιχράω, —, ἐπέχραον, attack, + *dat.*

ἔριφος, -ου, ὁ, young goat, kid

Ἔρυμας, -αντος, ὁ, Erymas

Ἰδομενεύς, -ῆος, ὁ, Idomeneus

κεάζω, —, ἐκέασσα, —, —, ἐκεάσθη, split, cleave

νέρθεν, beneath, below

πρήθω, —, ἔπρησα, spout; blow

ῥίς, ῥινός, ἡ, nose

σίντης, -ου, ravening

τινάσσω, —, ἐτίναξα, —, —, ἐτινάχθην, shake

Τρῶοι, -ων, οἱ, Trojans

χάσκω, —, χάνον, gape

Notes

346 **τό**: acc. pron. referring to στόμα

348 **τίναχθεν**: 3rd pl. aor. pass. indic. < τινάσσω, here "knocked out"

   ἐνέπλησθεν: 3rd pl. aor. pass. indic. < ἐμπίμπλημι

349 **αἵματος**: gen., after verb of filling

   τό: acc. pron. referring to αἵματος

351 **ἕκαστος**: although sing., working as a distributive adj. to modify the pl. noun ἡγεμόνες and the pl. verb ἕλον.

352–56 **ὡς . . . ὥς**: Notice the difference in accent, "just as . . . thus . . . "; this pair often marks the beginning and end of similes.

353 **αἱρεύμενοι**: Attic = αἱρούμενοι

   αἵ τ᾽: The gender of the flock is revealed. τε is untranslatable, as often after rel. prons.

   ὄρεσσι: dat. pl. < ὄρος

354 **ἀφραδίῃσι**: dat. of means, " . . . scattered by the folly of the shepherd"

   διέτμαγεν: 3rd pl. aor. pass.

   οἱ δέ: i.e., the wolves

357 **μνήσαντο**: < μιμνήσκω

   ἀλκῆς: partit. gen., regularly following verbs of remembering and forgetting

Making Sense of It (Continued)

345   Ἰδομενεὺς δ᾽ Ἐρύμαντα κατὰ στόμα νηλέϊ χαλκῷ

νύξε· τὸ δ᾽ ἀντικρὺ **δόρυ χάλκεον** ἐξεπέρησε

νέρθεν ὑπ᾽ ἐγκεφάλοιο, κέασσε δ᾽ ἄρ᾽ ὀστέα λευκά·

ἐκ δὲ τίναχθεν ὀδόντες, ἐνέπλησθεν δέ **οἱ ἄμφω**

αἵματος **ὀφθαλμοί·** τὸ δ᾽ ἀνὰ στόμα καὶ κατὰ ῥῖνας

350   πρῆσε χανών· θανάτου δὲ μέλαν νέφος ἀμφεκάλυψεν.

οὗτοι ἄρ᾽ ἡγεμόνες Δαναῶν ἕλον ἄνδρα ἕκαστος.

ὡς δὲ **λύκοι** ἄρνεσσιν ἐπέχραον ἢ ἐρίφοισι

σίνται, ὑπὲκ μήλων αἱρεύμενοι, αἵ τ᾽ ἐν ὄρεσσι

ποιμένος ἀφραδίῃσι διέτμαγεν· οἱ δὲ ἰδόντες

355   αἶψα διαρπάζουσιν ἀνάλκιδα θυμὸν ἐχούσας·

ὣς Δαναοὶ Τρώεσσιν ἐπέχραον· οἱ δὲ φόβοιο

δυσκελάδου μνήσαντο, λάθοντο δὲ **θούριδος ἀλκῆς.**

What Homer Actually Composed

Vocabulary

Αἴας, -αντος, ὁ, Ajax

Ἀκάμας, -αντος, ὁ, Acamas

βλάπτω, —, ἔβλαψα, —, —, ἐβλάβην, harm; catch, impede

δύω / δύνω, δύσω, ἔδυσα / ἔδυν, δέδυκα, sink

ἐρείπω, —, ἤριπα, throw down; *in aor.,* fall

θείνω, —, ἔθεινα, strike

ἱππόκομος, -η, -ον, with horse-hair crest

καρπάλιμος, -ον, swift

καυλός, -οῦ, ὁ, spear shaft; sword hilt

κιχάνω, κιχήσομαι, ἔκιχον, meet, reach

Κλεόβουλος, -ου, ὁ, Cleobulus

κλόνος, -ου, ὁ, confusion, panic of warfare

κωπήεις, -εσσα, -εν, hilted

Λύκων, -ονος, ὁ, Lycon

μέλεος, -η, -ον, vain, useless, empty

Μηριόνης, -εος, ὁ, Meriones

νύσσω, —, ἔνυξα, wound, pierce; thrust

Ὀϊλιάδης, -εος, ὁ, Ajax, son of Oeleus

ὄσσε, τώ, *dual,* eyes

οὔας, -ατος, τό, ear

ὄχεα, -ων, τά, *pl.,* chariot

παραείρω, —, —, —, —, παρηέρθην, detach; *in pass.,* hang down on one side

Πηνέλεως, ὁ, Peneleus

πλήσσω, —, ἔπληξα, πέπληγα, strike

πορφύρεος, -η, -ον, purple; gushing

ῥαίω, ῥαίσομαι, ἔραισα, —, —, ἐρραίσθην, shatter, break in pieces

συντρέχω, —, συνέδραμον, rush together

ὑποθερμαίνω, —, —, —, —, ὑπεθερμάνθην, *aor. pass.,* become heated

ὑπολύω, loose from under, undo

φάλος, -ου, ὁ, helmet device bearing a plume

Notes

330 **Αἴας . . . Ὀϊλιάδης:** There are two unrelated heroes named Ajax: the son of Telamon, and the son of Oeleus.

331 **ζωὸν ἔλε:** ENJAMBMENT of syntax across line boundaries is common in this passage. Why might that be so?

332 **ξίφει αὐχένα κωπήεντι:** Note the significant word arrangement; the sword continues through the neck. The second syllable of ξίφει is shortened by correption, and the line ending is spondaic.

335 **Πηνέλεως:** Although not a major figure in the *Iliad*, Peneleus does some heavy fighting in Books 14–16. How does Homer make him interesting? One means of judging the quality of a work of art is to examine the details, in this case, a minor character.

337 **τὼ δ᾿ αὖτις ξιφέεσσι:** In the initial stage of a formulaic battle exchange, the heroes launch their spears; if both combatants remain standing, hand-to-hand battle with swords ensues.

341 **ὑπέλυντο δὲ γυῖα:** This is a metrical adaptation of the common line ending λῦσε δὲ γυῖα (p. 79 line 12). Watch for other adaptations of formulaic language.

As It Was

330   Αἴας δὲ Κλεόβουλον Ὀϊλιάδης ἐπορούσας

ζωὸν ἕλε, βλαφθέντα κατὰ κλόνον· ἀλλά οἱ αὖθι

λῦσε μένος, πλήξας ξίφει αὐχένα κωπήεντι.

πᾶν δ᾽ ὑπεθερμάνθη ξίφος αἵματι· τὸν δὲ κατ᾽ ὄσσε

ἔλλαβε πορφύρεος θάνατος καὶ μοῖρα κραταιή.

335   Πηνέλεως δὲ Λύκων τε συνέδραμον· ἔγχεσι μὲν γὰρ

ἤμβροτον ἀλλήλων, μέλεον δ᾽ ἠκόντισαν ἄμφω·

τὼ δ᾽ αὖτις ξιφέεσσι συνέδραμον. ἔνθα Λύκων μὲν

ἱπποκόμου κόρυθος φάλον ἤλασεν, ἀμφὶ δὲ καυλὸν

φάσγανον ἐρραίσθη· ὁ δ᾽ ὑπ᾽ οὔατος αὐχένα θεῖνε

340   Πηνέλεως, πᾶν δ᾽ εἴσω ἔδυ ξίφος, ἔσχεθε δ᾽ οἶον

δέρμα, παρηέρθη δὲ κάρη, ὑπέλυντο δὲ γυῖα.

Μηριόνης δ᾽ Ἀκάμαντα κιχεὶς ποσὶ καρπαλίμοισι

νύξ᾽ ἵππων ἐπιβησόμενον κατὰ δεξιὸν ὦμον·

ἤριπε δ᾽ ἐξ ὀχέων, κατὰ δ᾽ ὀφθαλμῶν κέχυτ᾽ ἀχλύς.

Vocabulary

ἄναλκις, incapable of defense; unsuited for battle

ἀντικρύ, straight through

ἀφραδίη, -ης, ἡ, senselessness, recklessness

Δαναοί, -ῶν, οἱ, Danaans

διατμήγω, ——, διέτμηξα / διέτμαγον, ——, ——, διετμάγην, divide in two, sever

δυσκέλαδος, -ον, full of cries

ἐκπεράω, ——, ἐξεπέρησα, pass through

ἐπιχράω, ——, ἐπέχραον, attack, + *dat.*

ἔριφος, -ου, ὁ, young goat, kid

Ἔρυμας, -αντος, ὁ, Erymas

Ἰδομενεύς, -ῆος, ὁ, Idomeneus

κεάζω, ——, ἐκέασσα, ——, ——, ἐκεάσθη, split, cleave

νέρθεν, beneath, below

πρήθω, ——, ἔπρησα, spout; blow

ῥίς, ῥινός, ἡ, nose

σίντης, -ου, ravening

τινάσσω, ——, ἐτίναξα, ——, ——, ἐτινάχθην, shake

Τρῶοι, -ων, οἱ, Trojans

χάσκω, ——, χάνον, gape

Notes

345   νηλέϊ χαλκῷ: The phrase "pitiless bronze" exhibits both PROSOPOPOEIA and METONYMY. The prefix νη- is analogous to an initial alpha-privative (cf. Latin *non*), and appears prefixed to vowel-initial stems.

350   μέλαν νέφος ἀμφεκάλυψεν: Compare the line-ending at p. 81 line 325, σκότος ὄσσε κάλυψεν.

351   ἕλον ἄνδρα ἕκαστος: The conclusion of the scene echoes its beginning (ἀνὴρ ἕλεν ἄνδρα, p. 79 line 306).

352   ὡς δὲ λύκοι: What is the effect of using poetic SIMILES drawn from the natural world?

353   λύκοι . . . σίνται: By ENJAMBMENT of the adj., the predators "surround" the prey.

357   λάθοντο . . . θούριδος ἀλκῆς: The phrase displays CHIASMUS with the preceding φόβοιο/ δυσκελάδου μνήσαντο. Why is this device particularly effective here?

As It Was (Continued)

345 Ἰδομενεὺς δ᾽ Ἐρύμαντα κατὰ στόμα νηλέϊ χαλκῷ

νύξε· τὸ δ᾽ ἀντικρὺ δόρυ χάλκεον ἐξεπέρησε

νέρθεν ὑπ᾽ ἐγκεφάλοιο, κέασσε δ᾽ ἄρ᾽ ὀστέα λευκά·

ἐκ δὲ τίναχθεν ὀδόντες, ἐνέπλησθεν δέ οἱ ἄμφω

αἵματος ὀφθαλμοί· τὸ δ᾽ ἀνὰ στόμα καὶ κατὰ ῥῖνας

350 πρῆσε χανών· θανάτου δὲ μέλαν νέφος ἀμφεκάλυψεν.

οὗτοι ἄρ᾽ ἡγεμόνες Δαναῶν ἕλον ἄνδρα ἕκαστος.

ὡς δὲ λύκοι ἄρνεσσιν ἐπέχραον ἢ ἐρίφοισι

σίνται, ὑπὲκ μήλων αἰρεύμενοι, αἵ τ᾽ ἐν ὄρεσσι

ποιμένος ἀφραδίῃσι διέτμαγεν· οἱ δὲ ἰδόντες

355 αἶψα διαρπάζουσιν ἀνάλκιδα θυμὸν ἐχούσας·

ὣς Δαναοὶ Τρώεσσιν ἐπέχραον· οἱ δὲ φόβοιο

δυσκελάδου μνήσαντο, λάθοντο δὲ θούριδος ἀλκῆς.

AFTER READING WHAT HOMER COMPOSED

1. The depiction of violence in films, video games, and on television is a hotly debated topic. Are there substantial differences between seeing such violence and reading about it? What value is there in portraying deeply violent scenes in art and literature?

2. One expects to see images of wounding and death in a story about war. How does Homer keep us from reading through them so quickly that they lose their force?

READING 13

With His Final Words, Patroclus Prophesies Hector's Death

(*Iliad* 16.843–61)

BEFORE YOU READ WHAT HOMER COMPOSED

Introduction

Homer adds weight to his narrative by elaborating and expanding on traditional scenes: the more significant the event is, the longer the narrative expansion. Thus, Homer marks the death of important characters by extending their death scenes. The climactic death scene of Hector in Book 22 (Reading 15) takes a significant amount of time.

In Book 16, Patroclus demonstrates his heroic status by entering the battlefield and, in his own *aristeia* (see p. 54), slaughtering Trojans one after another. Even Sarpedon, the son of Zeus himself, loses his life at the hands of the advancing warrior. When Patroclus disobeys Achilles' command, however, and tries to attack the walls of Troy, Apollo intervenes and Patroclus dies by the combined blows of Euphorbus and Hector.

In this reading, Patroclus addresses his final words to the man who has mortally wounded him, and anticipates Hector's own death at the hands of Achilles.

Keep This Grammar in Mind — TENSE AND ASPECT

There are only three different times—past, present, and future—but there are *seven* verb tenses in Greek: present, imperfect, future, aorist, perfect, pluperfect, and future perfect. When a writer chooses a certain tense, it shows not only time, but also aspect. Aspect characterizes the progress of the action.

There are three aspects: simple, continuous, and completed. These combine with the past, present, and future to yield the Greek tenses. The aorist tense of an indicative verb shows an action that simply happened once in the past, while the imperfect tense shows a continuous or repeated past action. The perfect tense describes an action that happened in the past but, once completed, has an effect on the present. "I ate" (aorist) means that at a point in the past food was consumed. But "I have eaten," (perfect) although the action was completed in the past, implies "therefore I am now full."

Only indicative verbs show both time and aspect fully. An aorist indicative indicates both a past time and an aorist aspect; but an aorist infinitive, for example, may indicate aspect alone, without reference to a past action. The action of the infinitive in the sentence, "I will be willing to burn the village," is presumably meant to take place only once. The aorist aspect is therefore appropriate for the infinitive, even though the action is to take place in the future.

Stopping for Some Practice — TENSE AND ASPECT

You will encounter the following expressions in the reading selection below. Focus on the verbs and verbals (infinitives and participles). Based on the review of tense and aspect above, and your sense of the content of the passages, judge whether each boldfaced form represents a simple, completed, or continuous action. To review, take note also of augmented and unaugmented forms.

1. τὸν δ᾽ ὀλιγοδρανέων **προσέφης,** Πατρόκλεες ἱππεῦ· / "ἤδη νῦν, Ἕκτορ, μεγάλ᾽ **εὔχεο·"**

    Aspect: _____   Tense: _____

    Aspect: _____   Tense: _____

2. "σοὶ γὰρ **ἔδωκε** / νίκην Ζεὺς Κρονίδης καὶ Ἀπόλλων, οἵ με **δάμασσαν** / ῥηϊδίως· αὐτοὶ γὰρ ἀπ᾽ ὤμων τεύχε᾽ **ἕλοντο."**

    Aspect: _____   Tense: _____

    Aspect: _____   Tense: _____

    Aspect: _____   Tense: _____

3. ὣς ἄρα μιν **εἰπόντα** τέλος θανάτοιο **κάλυψε·**

    Aspect: _____   Tense: _____

    Aspect: _____   Tense: _____

4. τὸν καὶ **τεθνηῶτα** προσηύδα φαίδιμος Ἕκτωρ· / "Πατρόκλεις, τί νύ μοι μαντεύεαι αἰπὺν ὄλεθρον;"

    Aspect: _____   Tense: _____

5. "τίς δ᾽ οἶδ᾽ εἴ κ᾽ Ἀχιλεὺς, Θέτιδος πάϊς ἠϋκόμοιο, / φθήῃ ἐμῷ ὑπὸ δουρὶ **τυπεὶς** ἀπὸ θυμὸν **ὀλέσσαι;"**

    Aspect: _____   Tense: _____

    Aspect: _____   Tense: _____

HELPING YOU READ WHAT HOMER COMPOSED

Vocabulary

ἀντιβολέω, ἀντιβολήσω, ἀντεβόλησα, meet, encounter

Ἀπόλλων, -ωνος, ὁ, Apollo

αὐτόθι, on the spot; immediately

εἴκοσι(ν), twenty

Ἕκτωρ, -ορος, ὁ, Hector

ἐξεναρίζω, ἐξεναρίξω, ἐξενάριξα, strip of armor; kill

Εὔφορβος, -ου, ὁ, Euphorbus

Ζεύς, Διός, ὁ, Zeus

ἱππεύς, -ῆος, ὁ, chariot-fighter

Κρονίδης, -εος, ὁ, son of Cronus

Λητώ, -οῦς, ἡ, Leto

νίκη, -ης, ἡ, victory

ὀλιγοδρανέων, *pple. only,* powerless, weak

Πατρόκλος, -ῆος, ὁ, Patroclus

Notes

843   **προσέφης:** 2nd sing. aor. < πρόσφημι

    Πατρόκλεες ἱππεῦ: voc.; the poet speaks directly to Patroclus at a moment of high emotion

844   **μεγάλ᾿:** neut. acc., used as adv., "boast loudly . . ."

    εὔχεο: 2nd sing. imperat.

    ἔδωκε: aor. < δίδωμι

846   **αὐτοί:** nom. always emphatic; here reinforcing Patroclus' assessment of Hector's accomplishment

    ἕλοντο: < αἱρέω; the mid. generally means "choose," but here retains its root meaning, "take (for themselves)"

847   **τοιοῦτοι:** The implicit comparison is to Hector himself; without divine intervention, Patroclus claims, he could have slain twenty men like Hector.

    ἐείκοσιν: variant of εἴκοσι(ν)

847–48   **ἀντεβόλησαν . . . ὄλοντο:** mixed contrary-to-fact condition with aor. in the protasis and impf. + κε in the apodosis, "even if twenty such men *had* attacked me, they all *would now be* dead . . ."

848   **ὄλοντο:** aor. < ὄλλυμι

    δαμέντες: aor. pass. pple. < δαμάζω

849   **ἔκτανεν:** aor. < κτείνω

850   **ἀνδρῶν:** partit. gen.

As You Read

1. To whom does Patroclus attribute his defeat?

2. Watch for the following literary devices: ALLITERATION in *p*; ASSONANCE in *a*; ENJAMBMENT. How do they heighten the emotion in these lines?

3. Hiatus (p. xviii) occurs 6 times in these lines (846, 848, 852, 856, 859, and 861), and correption twice (852, 861). What is the effect of the frequent occurrence of these metrical peculiarities?

Summary

Patroclus' death scene extends over many lines. Apollo, with a firm blow to the back, disarms him of his shield and helmet, the Trojan Euphorbus strikes him with a spear from behind, and only then does Hector deal the death blow.

As Patroclus dies, he reminds Hector that he has not killed him on his own, and boasts that he could kill twenty men such as Hector. Patroclus also warns Hector that his death at Achilles' hands is near. Hector replies that it may be Achilles who is slain when they meet.

Making Sense of It

τὸν δ᾽ (Ἕκτορα) ὀλιγοδρανέων προσέφης, Πατρόκλεες ἱππεῦ·

"ἤδη νῦν, Ἕκτορ, μεγάλ(α) εὔχεο· σοὶ γὰρ ἔδωκε

845   νίκην Ζεὺς Κρονίδης καὶ Ἀπόλλων, οἵ με δάμασσαν

ῥηϊδίως· αὐτοὶ γὰρ ἀπ᾽ ὤμων τεύχε(α) ἕλοντο.

τοιοῦτοι δ᾽ (ἄνδρες) εἴ πέρ μοι ἐείκοσιν ἀντεβόλησαν,

πάντες κ(ε) αὐτόθ(ι) ὄλοντο ἐμῷ ὑπὸ **δουρὶ** δαμέντες.

ἀλλά με μοῖρ(α) ὀλοὴ καὶ Λητοῦς ἔκτανεν υἱός,

850   ἀνδρῶν δ᾽ Εὔφορβος· σὺ δέ με τρίτος ἐξεναρίζεις.

Vocabulary

ἄγχι, near

Αἰακίδης, -αο, ὁ, descendant of Aeacus, i.e., Achilles

Ἀϊδόσδε, to(ward) Hades

Ἀχιλεύς, -ῆος, ὁ, Achilles

βείομαι, live

γοάω, γοήσομαι, weep, wail

δηρός, -ή, -όν, *of time,* long

ἥβη, -ης, ἡ, youth

Θέτις, -ιδος, ἡ, Thetis

θην, *affirmative particle, often with ironic force*

κραταιός, -ή, -όν, strong, powerful

μαντεύω, μαντεύσομαι, prophesy

πέτομαι, ——, ἐπτάμην, fly

ποτμός, -οῦ, ὁ, fate, doom

ῥέθεα, -ων, τά, limbs

τύπτω, ——, ἐτύψα, ——, ——, ἐτύπην, strike, beat

φαίδιμος, -η, -ον, brilliant, bright

φθάνω, φθήσομαι, ἔφθην, be first, anticipate, + *pple.*

Notes

852   αὐτός: emphatic, "you yourself"

      βέῃ: 2ⁿᵈ sing. pres. used with fut. force

853   παρέστηκεν: aor. < παρίστημι

854   δαμέντ᾽: dat. sing. with τοι in line 852

855   θανάτοιο: subjective gen. (p. 26); death would be the subject of the verbal action implied by τέλος

856   βεβήκει: plpf. < βαίνω

857   ὅν: functioning as a possess. adj.

858   καί: concessive, "even though Patroclus had . . . "

859   Πατρόκλεις: cf. the uncontracted voc. in line 843

861   φθήῃ: 3ʳᵈ sing. aor. act. subjnc. < φθάνω

      τυπείς: aor. pass.; the pple. with φθάνω expresses what will be experienced first

      ἀπὸ . . . ὀλέσσαι: adverbial ἀπό with ὀλέσσαι, as though < ἀπόλλυμι; here transitive, taking the obj. θυμόν

Making Sense of It (Continued)

ἄλλο δέ τοι ἐρέω, σὺ δ᾽ ἐνὶ **φρεσὶ** βάλλεο **σῇσιν·**

οὔ θην οὐδ᾽ αὐτὸς δηρὸν βέῃ, ἀλλά τοι ἤδη

ἄγχι παρέστηκεν θάνατος καὶ μοῖρα κραταιή

χερσὶ δαμέντ(ι) **Ἀχιλῆος ἀμύμονος Αἰακίδαο.**"

855   ὣς ἄρα **μιν εἰπόντα** τέλος θανάτοιο κάλυψε·

ψυχὴ δ᾽ ἐκ ῥεθέων **πταμένη** Ἀϊδόσδε βεβήκει,

ὃν πότμον **γοόωσα, λιποῦσ(α)** ἀνδροτῆτα καὶ ἥβην.

τὸν (Πατρόκλεα) καὶ τεθνηῶτα προσηύδα φαίδιμος Ἕκτωρ

"Πατρόκλεις, τί νύ μοι μαντεύεαι αἰπὺν ὄλεθρον;

860   τίς δ᾽ οἶδ(ε) εἴ κ᾽ **Ἀχιλεὺς,** Θέτιδος **πάϊς** ἠϋκόμοιο,

φθήῃ **ἐμῷ** ὑπὸ **δουρὶ** τυπεὶς ἀπὸ θυμὸν ὀλέσσαι;"

WHAT HOMER ACTUALLY COMPOSED

Vocabulary

ἄγχι, near

Αἰακίδης, -αο, ὁ, descendant of Aeacus, i.e., Achilles

Ἀϊδόσδε, to(ward) Hades

ἀντιβολέω, ἀντιβολήσω, ἀντεβόλησα, meet, encounter

Ἀπόλλων, -ωνος, ὁ, Apollo

αὐτόθι, on the spot; immediately

Ἀχιλεύς, -ῆος, ὁ, Achilles

βείομαι, live

γοάω, γοήσομαι, weep, wail

δηρός, -ή, -όν, of time, long

εἴκοσι(ν), twenty

Ἕκτωρ, -ορος, ὁ, Hector

ἐξεναρίζω, ἐξεναρίξω, ἐξενάριξα, strip of armor; kill

Εὔφορβος, -ου, ὁ, Euphorbus

Ζεύς, Διός, ὁ, Zeus

ἥβη, -ης, ἡ, youth

Θέτις, -ιδος, ἡ, Thetis

θην, *affirmative particle, often with ironic force*

ἱππεύς, -ῆος, ὁ, chariot-fighter

κραταιός, -ή, -όν, strong, powerful

Κρονίδης, -εος, ὁ, son of Cronus

Λητώ, -οῦς, ἡ, Leto

μαντεύω, μαντεύσομαι, prophesy

νίκη, -ης, ἡ, victory

ὀλιγοδρανέων, *pple. only*, powerless, weak

Πατρόκλος, -ῆος, ὁ, Patroclus

πέτομαι, —, ἐπτάμην, fly

ποτμός, -οῦ, ὁ, fate, doom

ῥέθεα, -ων, τά, limbs

τύπτω, —, ἔτυψα, —, —, ἐτύπην, strike, beat

φαίδιμος, -η, -ον, brilliant, bright

φθάνω, φθήσομαι, ἔφθην, be first, anticipate, + *pple.*

Notes

843   **Πατρόκλεες:** The poet's direct address to Patroclus is a form of APOSTROPHE.

845   **νίκην:** The poet uses ENJAMBMENT well in the opening two lines of this speech to underscore Patroclus' urgency in his dying breaths. This has the effect of drawing the listener/reader into the scene. Look for other literary devices that highlight the importance of Patroclus' speech.

846   **ἕλοντο:** The middle voice may stress to Hector that the gods had their own interest in seeing Patroclus fall.

847–48   **τοιοῦτοι . . . δαμέντες:** Patroclus asserts his conviction and determination with HYPERBOLE.

849–50   **μοῖρ᾽ . . . Εὔφορβος:** Patroclus diminishes Hector's glory by crediting others with his death.

854   **Αἰακίδαο:** Achilles was the paternal grandson of Aeacus.

As It Was

τὸν δ᾽ ὀλιγοδρανέων προσέφης, Πατρόκλεες ἱππεῦ·

"ἤδη νῦν, Ἕκτορ, μεγάλ᾽ εὔχεο· σοὶ γὰρ ἔδωκε

845   νίκην Ζεὺς Κρονίδης καὶ Ἀπόλλων, οἵ με δάμασσαν

ῥηϊδίως· αὐτοὶ γὰρ ἀπ᾽ ὤμων τεύχε᾽ ἕλοντο.

τοιοῦτοι δ᾽ εἴ πέρ μοι ἐείκοσιν ἀντεβόλησαν,

πάντες κ᾽ αὐτόθ᾽ ὄλοντο ἐμῷ ὑπὸ δουρὶ δαμέντες.

ἀλλά με μοῖρ᾽ ὀλοὴ καὶ Λητοῦς ἔκτανεν υἱός,

850   ἀνδρῶν δ᾽ Εὔφορβος· σὺ δέ με τρίτος ἐξεναρίζεις.

ἄλλο δέ τοι ἐρέω, σὺ δ᾽ ἐνὶ φρεσὶ βάλλεο σῇσιν·

οὔ θην οὐδ᾽ αὐτὸς δηρὸν βέῃ, ἀλλά τοι ἤδη

ἄγχι παρέστηκεν θάνατος καὶ μοῖρα κραταιή,

χερσὶ δαμέντ᾽ Ἀχιλῆος ἀμύμονος Αἰακίδαο."

855   ὣς ἄρα μιν εἰπόντα τέλος θανάτοιο κάλυψε·

ψυχὴ δ᾽ ἐκ ῥεθέων πταμένη Ἀϊδόσδε βεβήκει,

ὃν πότμον γοόωσα, λιποῦσ᾽ ἀνδροτῆτα καὶ ἥβην.

τὸν καὶ τεθνηῶτα προσηύδα φαίδιμος Ἕκτωρ·

"Πατρόκλεις, τί νύ μοι μαντεύεαι αἰπὺν ὄλεθρον;

860   τίς δ᾽ οἶδ᾽ εἴ κ᾽ Ἀχιλεὺς, Θέτιδος πάϊς ἠϋκόμοιο,

φθήῃ ἐμῷ ὑπὸ δουρὶ τυπεὶς ἀπὸ θυμὸν ὀλέσσαι;"

AFTER READING WHAT HOMER COMPOSED

1.   What do the speeches in this scene tell us about Patroclus and Hector?

2.   Why would the poet have Hector strike the third blow?

3.   Patroclus says that Moira is responsible for his death. Look up Moira to get a sense of the role she plays in Greek ideas about life and death. Can we reconcile the activity of Apollo and the role of fate in Patroclus' death?

READING 14

Achilles Expresses Regret

(*Iliad* 18.97–116)

BEFORE YOU READ WHAT HOMER COMPOSED

Introduction

Achilles now understands the consequences of his withdrawal from the battlefield: Hector has killed Patroclus, his closest friend. Turning to his mother for comfort, Achilles bemoans his failure to protect his friend. His recognition of the effects of his anger pushes him toward a deeper self-awareness. The question remains whether he will undergo a real transformation of character.

Keep This Grammar in Mind — COMPARATIVES AND SUPERLATIVES

Comparative and superlative adjectives usually have a reference point. Consider the sentence, "Telamonian Ajax is larger than Oelean Ajax." It is clear that Ajax the Great is compared specifically to the lesser Ajax. Again, when Achilles claims to be "the best of the Achaeans," it is specifically in reference to the Achaeans that Achilles claims to be best.

Comparatives and superlatives do not always have a clear point of reference. An author may simply say that a person is *rather* large, or *extremely* large. These thoughts are also represented by comparatives and superlatives. Possible translations for the comparative degree are "rather," "fairly," or "quite." For the superlative degree, one might use "extremely," "very," or "too."

Stopping for Some Practice— COMPARATIVE AND SUPERLATIVE ADJECTIVES

Two of these sentences you have previously read and two you will encounter in this reading. Note the force of the boldfaced adjectives. Write the degree of each, and the positive degree word on which it is based.

1. Ἀτρεΐδη **κύδιστε, φιλοκτεανώτατε** πάντων,
   πῶς γάρ τοι δώσουσι γέρας μεγάθυμοι Ἀχαιοί;

   Degree _____

   Positive Degree _____

   Degree _____

   Positive Degree _____

2. Φυλεΐδης δ᾽ Ἄμφικλον ἐφορμηθέντα δοκεύσας
   ἔφθη ὀρεξάμενος πρυμνὸν σκέλος, ἔνθα **πάχιστος**.

   Degree _____

   Positive Degree _____

3. . . . ἀγορῇ δέ τ᾽ **ἀμείνονές** εἰσι καὶ ἄλλοι.

   Degree _____

   Positive Degree _____

4. [χόλος] . . . πολὺ **γλυκίων** μέλιτος καταλειβομένοιο
   ἀνδρῶν ἐν στήθεσσιν ἀέξεται . . .

   Degree _____

   Positive Degree _____

WHAT HOMER ACTUALLY COMPOSED

Vocabulary

ἀλκτήρ, -ῆρος, ὁ, defender

ἄχνυμαι, be grieved, be troubled

δαμάζω, δαμῶ, ἐδάμα(σ)σα, ——, δέδμημαι, ἐδμήθην, tame, overcome

ἐπαμύνω, defend, rescue

ἐτώσιος, -ον, vain, worthless

ἐφίημι, ἐφήσω, ἐφῆκα, incite

ἧμαι, sit, be seated

καταλείβω, drip

κήρ, κηρός, ἡ, fate, death

κιχάνω, overtake, reach

μέλι, -ιτος, τό, honey

νέομαι, go, come; return

ὀλετήρ, -ῆρος, ὁ, destroyer, slayer

ὀχθέω, ——, ὤχθησα, be troubled, be angry

προτεύχω, ——, ——, ——, προτέτυχμαι, let go forth, let pass

τελέω, τελέω, ἐτέλε(σ)σα, ——, τετέλσμαι, ἐτελέσθην, accomplish, fulfill

τηλόθι, + *gen.*, far away from

φάος, -ου, τό, light

φθίω, φθίσω, ἔφθισα, ——, ἔφθιμαι, ἐφθίθην, waste away, perish

χαλεπαίνω, act in rage

Notes

98   τεθναίην: opt. of wish < θνήσκω; with a single word, Achilles demonstrates the depth of his sorrow, frustration, and anger at the loss of his friend.

100   ἐμεῖο: gen., as regularly with verbs of lacking or needing

δῆσεν: aor. < δέω

ἀλκτῆρα: predicate acc. with the infin.; takes gen. ἄρης, "defender from . . ."

102   φάος: figuratively, "the light of deliverance"

103   πολέες: < πολύς

δάμεν: 3rd pl. aor. pass. < δαμάζω

Ἕκτορι δίῳ: Homer uses dat. for a personal agent. How would agency be expressed in Attic Greek?

104   ἐτώσιον ἄχθος ἀρούρης: predicate to Achilles, "a weight of/on the earth"

105   τοῖος ἐὼν οἷος: concessive, "even though I am such as . . ."

105–106:   Excellence in battle and debate define Homer's heroic code.

107   ὡς . . . ἀπόλοιτο: opt. of wish

ἔρις: Later tradition traces the origin of the Trojan war to the appearance of Eris, goddess of strife, at the marriage of Achilles' parents, Peleus and Thetis.

108   ἐφέηκε: aor. < ἐφίημι

πολύφρονά περ: concessive

χαλεπῆναι: aor. infin.

109   γλυκίων: compar. < γλυκίος

μέλιτος καταλειβομένοιο: gen. of comparison

112   ἐάσομεν: aor. subjnc., "Let us allow . . ."

περ: = καίπερ

114   κιχείω: irregular aor. subjnc. < κιχάνω

115–16   ὁππότε κεν . . . ἐθέλῃ: indefinite rel. clause

As You Read

1.   Watch for words and phrases that highlight the grief and anger that Achilles confronts.

2.   Speech and action are central to the heroic code. How does the poet convey their importance?

Summary

Achilles complains to his mother, the goddess Thetis, about the dreadful nature of anger. He grudgingly sets aside his rage against Agamemnon and resolves to kill Hector.

As It Was

τὴν δὲ μέγ᾽ ὀχθήσας προσέφη πόδας ὠκὺς Ἀχιλλεύς·

"αὐτίκα τεθναίην, ἐπεὶ οὐκ ἄρ᾽ ἔμελλον ἑταίρῳ

κτεινομένῳ ἐπαμῦναι· ὁ μὲν μάλα τηλόθι πάτρης

100   ἔφθιτ᾽, ἐμεῖο δὲ δῆσεν ἀρῆς ἀλκτῆρα γενέσθαι.

νῦν δ᾽ ἐπεὶ οὐ νέομαί γε φίλην ἐς πατρίδα γαῖαν,

οὐδέ τι Πατρόκλῳ γενόμην φάος οὐδ᾽ ἑτάροισι

τοῖς ἄλλοις, οἳ δὴ πολέες δάμεν Ἕκτορι δίῳ,

ἀλλ᾽ ἧμαι παρὰ νηυσὶν ἐτώσιον ἄχθος ἀρούρης,

105   τοῖος ἐὼν οἷος οὔ τις Ἀχαιῶν χαλκοχιτώνων

ἐν πολέμῳ· ἀγορῇ δέ τ᾽ ἀμείνονές εἰσι καὶ ἄλλοι.

ὡς ἔρις ἔκ τε θεῶν ἔκ τ᾽ ἀνθρώπων ἀπόλοιτο,

καὶ χόλος, ὅς τ᾽ ἐφέηκε πολύφρονά περ χαλεπῆναι,

ὅς τε πολὺ γλυκίων μέλιτος καταλειβομένοιο

110   ἀνδρῶν ἐν στήθεσσιν ἀέξεται ἠΰτε καπνός·

ὡς ἐμὲ νῦν ἐχόλωσεν ἄναξ ἀνδρῶν Ἀγαμέμνων.

ἀλλὰ τὰ μὲν προτετύχθαι ἐάσομεν ἀχνύμενοί περ,

θυμὸν ἐνὶ στήθεσσι φίλον δαμάσαντες ἀνάγκῃ·

νῦν δ᾽ εἶμ᾽, ὄφρα φίλης κεφαλῆς ὀλετῆρα κιχείω,

115   Ἕκτορα· κῆρα δ᾽ ἐγὼ τότε δέξομαι, ὁππότε κεν δὴ

Ζεὺς ἐθέλῃ τελέσαι ἠδ᾽ ἀθάνατοι θεοὶ ἄλλοι."

AFTER READING WHAT HOMER COMPOSED

1. How does Homer explore the idea of a hero in these lines? What poetic devices do you notice?

2. What might be the significance, if any, of calling Achilles "swift-footed" in line 97 of this passage?

3. Do you find Achilles' change of heart credible? Why or why not?

READING 15

Achilles Kills Hector

(*Iliad* 22.306–30)

What Homer Actually Composed

Vocabulary

ἄγριος, -α, -ον, wild, fierce, savage

ἀμαλός, -ή, -όν, tender, gentle; feeble

ἔθειραι, -ων, αἱ, horse-hair; plume of a helmet

εἴλω, —, ἔελσα, —, ἐέλμαι, ἐάλην, crowd together, hem in; *mid./pass.,* crouch

ἐμπίπλημι, ἐμπλήσω, ἐνέπλησα, fill

ἐρύω, ἐρύω, εἴρυ(σ)σα, —, εἴρυσμαι, draw, pull

θαμέες, θαμειαί, *pl.,* set close together, thick; frequent

λαπάρη, -ης, ἡ, hollow under the ribs, flank

νέφος, -εος, τό, cloud, mist

οἰμάω, —, οἴμησα, spring upon

περισσείω, wave about

πρόσθεν, before; + *gen.,* before, in front of

πτώξ, -ωκός, ὁ, cowering, timid

στιβαρός, -ή, -όν, heavy, stout

τείνω, τενῶ, ἔτεινα, τέτακα, —, ἐτάθην, stretch, strain

τετραφάλος, -όν, with four plumes

φάσγανον, -ου, τό, sword

φωνέω, —, ἐφώνησα, speak

Notes

306 φωνήσας: Hector has just finished speaking.

307 τό: i.e., Hector's sword; scan as long syllable

οἱ: "his"

τέτατο: plpf. pass. < τείνω; the sword had been strapped at Hector's side

308 ἀλείς: aor. pple. < εἴλω; Hector crouches poised to strike, and then hurls himself toward Achilles

ὡς: introduces a simile describing Hector; the accent in the text is from the enclitic

308–309 ὥς τ᾽ . . . ὅς τ᾽: Each τε is untranslatable, a Homeric standard following a rel. pron.

εἶσιν: < εἶμι; note the accent

310 ἁρπάξων: fut. pple. showing intention

311 ὥς: closes the simile, "just so Hector . . ."; note the accent

312 μένεος: gen., as regularly with verbs of filling

313 κάλυψε: takes acc. of item used for protective cover, i.e., σάκος

315 τετραφάλῳ: Compound adjs. have only two terminations, with no separate fem. endings.

316 Ἥφαιστος: Achilles had been without his armor, which Hector stripped from Patroclus; he goes into battle here with a newly made divine panoply.

ἵει: < ἵημι, here "applied to"

θαμειάς: modifies the rel. pron., which refers to ἔθειραι

Summary

The death of Hector is by no means the end of the poem, but it is clearly the point at which the action reaches its zenith. Achilles has not yet given his anger full vent. In his previous dealings with the Achaeans, even with Agamemnon, he stopped short of fulfilling his desire to avenge himself for the dishonor he had been dealt. The death of Patroclus pushes Achilles over the edge to action, and he will not rest until he has glutted his fury by killing Hector and defiling his corpse.

Achilles and Hector enter battle. Hector is killed.

As It Was

ὣς ἄρα φωνήσας εἰρύσσατο φάσγανον ὀξύ,

τό οἱ ὑπὸ λαπάρην τέτατο μέγα τε στιβαρόν τε,

οἴμησεν δὲ ἀλεὶς ὥς τ᾽ αἰετὸς ὑψιπετήεις,

ὅς τ᾽ εἶσιν πεδίονδε διὰ νεφέων ἐρεβεννῶν

310   ἁρπάξων ἢ ἄρν᾽ ἀμαλὴν ἢ πτῶκα λαγωόν·

ὣς Ἕκτωρ οἴμησε τινάσσων φάσγανον ὀξύ.

ὁρμήθη δ᾽ Ἀχιλεύς, μένεος δ᾽ ἐμπλήσατο θυμὸν

ἀγρίου, πρόσθεν δὲ σάκος στέρνοιο κάλυψε

καλὸν δαιδάλεον, κόρυθι δ᾽ ἐπένευε φαεινῇ

315   τετραφάλῳ· καλαὶ δὲ περισσείοντο ἔθειραι

χρύσεαι, ἃς Ἥφαιστος ἵει λόφον ἀμφὶ θαμειάς.

Vocabulary

ἀμολγός, -οῦ, ὁ, gloom, darkness

ἀσφάραγος, -ου, ὁ, windpipe

αὐχήν, -ένος, ὁ, neck

εἴκω, ——, εἶξα, *of fighting,* yield; withdraw from, + gen.

ἐρείπω, ἐρείψω, ἤριπον, ἐρήριπα, ——, ἠρείφθην, throw down; aor. fall

εὐήκης, -ες, sharp-pointed

κατακτείνω, κατακτενῶ, κατέκτανον, ——, ——, κατεκτάθην, kill, slay

λαυκανίη, -ης, ἡ, throat

μέμαα, *only pf.,* be eager, contend

πάλλω, ——, πῆλα, shake, brandish; hurl

προσεῖπον, spoke to, addressed

χρώς, χροός / χρωτός, ὁ, flesh, skin

Notes

319 ἀπέλαμπ᾿: here, impersonal, "just so light shone from . . . "

320 δεξιτερῇ: used as substantive, "with his right hand"

φρονέων κακόν: "contriving evil"

321 εἴξειε: aor. opt. < εἴκω; indefinite rel. clause, " . . . where the skin might give way"

322 τοῦ: i.e., Hector's skin

ἄλλο τόσον μέν: "in (respect to) every other part . . . "

323 Πατρόκλοιο: subjective gen.

βίην: obj. of κατακτάς

324 φαίνετο δ᾿: answers μέν, two lines above

325 ὤκιστος: superl. < ὠκύς

326 τῇ: "there, in that place"

οἷ: reflex. pron.

μεμαῶτ᾿: acc., referring to Hector

ἔλασ᾿: < ἐλαύνω

327 ἤλυθ᾿: aor. < ἔρχομαι

328 ἀπ᾿: adv., by TMESIS

τάμε: aor. < τέμνω

329 τί: indefinite, accent from following enclitic

προτιείποι: opt. in secondary sequence, following past tense main verb, τάμε; Hector falls, but does not die instantly.

330 ὅ: neut. acc., as accented, referring to the speech Achilles is about to deliver; but accents have no strong manuscript authority, and the word has been read elsewhere as unaccented, i.e., as a definite article with Achilles.

As It Was (Continued)

οἷος δ᾽ ἀστὴρ εἶσι μετ᾽ ἀστράσι νυκτὸς ἀμολγῷ

ἕσπερος, ὃς κάλλιστος ἐν οὐρανῷ ἵσταται ἀστήρ,

ὣς αἰχμῆς ἀπέλαμπ᾽ εὐήκεος, ἣν ἄρ᾽ Ἀχιλλεὺς

320 πάλλεν δεξιτερῇ φρονέων κακὸν Ἕκτορι δίῳ,

εἰσορόων χρόα καλόν, ὅπῃ εἴξειε μάλιστα.

τοῦ δὲ καὶ ἄλλο τόσον μὲν ἔχε χρόα χάλκεα τεύχεα,

καλά, τὰ Πατρόκλοιο βίην ἐνάριξε κατακτάς·

φαίνετο δ᾽ ᾗ κληῖδες ἀπ᾽ ὤμων αὐχέν᾽ ἔχουσι,

325 λαυκανίην, ἵνα τε ψυχῆς ὤκιστος ὄλεθρος·

τῇ ῥ᾽ ἐπὶ οἷ μεμαῶτ᾽ ἔλασ᾽ ἔγχεῖ δῖος Ἀχιλλεύς,

ἀντικρὺ δ᾽ ἁπαλοῖο δι᾽ αὐχένος ἤλυθ᾽ ἀκωκή·

οὐδ᾽ ἄρ᾽ ἀπ᾽ ἀσφάραγον μελίη τάμε χαλκοβάρεια,

ὄφρα τί μιν προτιείποι ἀμειβόμενος ἐπέεσσιν.

330 ἤριπε δ᾽ ἐν κονίῃς· ὁ δ᾽ ἐπεύξατο δῖος Ἀχιλλεύς . . .

AFTER READING WHAT HOMER COMPOSED

1. Why does Homer mention that Hector was wearing the armor he stripped from Patroclus?

2. How does word order augment the poetry in lines 312 and 313? Find other significant examples.

The grounding that you have acquired in epic forms, grammar, and vocabulary, and your under-standing of the literary qualities of Homer's verse, will allow you to continue reading epic poetry with increasing enjoyment. Although it will take a long time to read through the *Iliad* and *Odyssey*, you will certainly be able to achieve that goal. Ancient Greek epic is not confined to Homer's poetry. Perhaps you will also be interested in Hesiod's story of the origins of the gods, told in his *Theogony*. Whatever you choose to read, your pleasure and sense of accomplishment will more than repay the effort necessary to finish the epics. Take your time and enjoy them. Καλὴ τύχη!

APPENDIX A

Figures of Speech

The following are names, definitions, and examples of a number of "verbal tools" used to emphasize or reinforce words, images, and concepts of importance. You probably have studied some of these and others in your work with English literature. These verbal tools are variously referred to as figures of speech, literary figures, literary devices, aphorisms, and by other terms; their definitions are notoriously imprecise, and inconsistently classified from one source to another. As you study these terms, their definitions, and the examples provided, note that many of their names are Greek in origin.

ALLITERATION: the emphatic repetition of initial consonant sounds in a word group

> **χύντο χαμαὶ χολάδες,** τὸν δὲ σκότος ὄσσε κάλυψε.
> "His bowels poured out on the ground, and darkness covered his eyes." (4.526)

ANACOLUTHON (APOSIOPESIS): an abrupt breaking off in mid-sentence, indicating an animated emotional response

> αἴθ᾿ ὄφελες σὺ μὲν αὖθι μετ᾿ ἀθανάτης ἁλίῃσι
> ναίειν, Πηλεὺς δὲ θνητὴν ἀγαγέσθαι ἄκοιτιν.
> **νῦν δ᾿—**ἵνα καὶ σοὶ πένθος ἐνὶ φρεσὶ μυρίον εἴη
> παιδὸς ἀποφθιμένοιο, τὸν οὐχ ὑποδέξεαι αὖτις
> οἴκαδε νοστήσαντ᾿ . . .

> "If only you were living there with the immortal sea nymphs,
> and Peleus had taken a mortal wife.
> But now—that you might have in your heart the boundless grief
> of a vanished child, whom you will not receive again
> as he returns home . . . " (18.86–90)

ANAPHORA: the repetition of the same word or phrase at the beginnings of successive word groups

> **ἦμος δ᾿** ἠέλιος κατέδυ καὶ ἐπὶ κνέφας ἦλθε,
> δὴ τότε κοιμήσαντο παρὰ πρυμνήσια νηός·
> **ἦμος δ᾿** ἠριγένεια φάνη ῥοδοδάκτυλος Ἠώς,
> καὶ τότ᾿ ἔπειτ᾿ ἀνάγοντο μετὰ στρατὸν εὐρὺν Ἀχαιῶν·

> "**And when** the sun set and darkness came on,
> then they reclined beside the stern cables of the ship;
> **and when** early-born, rosy-fingered Dawn appeared,
> indeed then they put to sea toward the wide army of the Achaeans . . . " (1.475–78)

ANASTROPHE: the transposing of normal or expected word order

οὐ μὰν ἀκλεέες **Λυκίην κάτα** κοιρανέουσιν
ἡμέτεροι βασιλῆες . . .

"Indeed not without glory **in Lycia** do
our kings rule . . . " (12.318–19)

τὸν δ᾽ **ὡς** οὖν ἐνόησεν Ἀλέξανδρος θεοειδὴς
ἐν προμάχοισι φανέντα, κατεπλήγη φίλον ἦτορ . . .

"But **when** godlike Alexander recognized **him**
as he appeared among the foremost in battle, he was dismayed as to his heart . . . " (3.30–31)

APOSTROPHE: speech of a character to one not present, or speech of the omniscient narrator to an internal character

τὸν δ᾽ ὀλιγοδρανέων προσέφης, **Πατρόκλεες ἱππεῦ·**

"But feebly you spoke to him, **horseman Patroclus . . .** " (16.843)

ASSONANCE: the emphatic repetition of initial and/or internal vowel sounds in a word group

τὴν δ᾽ **ἠμείβετ᾽ ἔπειτα φιλομμειδὴς** Ἀφροδίτη· (5.375)

"and then Aphrodite lover of laughter answered her . . . "

CHIASMUS: a mirrored, or "A-B-B-A" word arrangement, within a line or across the line boundary; it may be "pure" (i.e., consist strictly of four elements), or more complex (i.e., contain one or more other words, sometimes yielding an A-B-C-B-A arrangement)

Πάτροκλος δ᾽ ἵπποισι καὶ Αὐτομέδοντι **κελεύσας** . . .

"And Patroclus, urging on his horses and Automedon . . . " (16.684)

ENJAMBMENT: the continuation of a thought or sense unit beyond the end of a line of poetry, allowing the poet to sustain dramatic effect and mediating the artificiality of measured verse

Ἕκτορ ἀτάρ που ἔφης Πατροκλῆ᾽ ἐξεναρίζων
σῶς ἔσσεσθ᾽, ἐμὲ δ᾽ οὐδὲν ὀπίζεο νόσφιν ἐόντα,
νήπιε·

"But Hector, you said, as you were stripping Patroclus of armor,
that you would be safe, and did not have awe of me, as I was far away,
you fool . . . " (22.331–33)

EPITHET: an adjective or appositive noun that attributes a precise or unique quality

ἀλλ᾽ ὅτε δή ῥ᾽ ἵκανον ὅθι **ξανθὸς** Μενέλαος
βλήμενος ἦν . . .

"But when they arrived where **yellow-haired** Menelaus,
who had been struck, was . . . " (4.210–11)

τὸν δ᾽ αὖτε προσέειπεν **ἄναξ ἀνδρῶν** Ἀγαμέμνων·

And Agamemnon, **lord of men,** addressed him in reply . . . " (9.114)

HENDIADYS: the use of two nouns with the same or similar meaning, linked by a conjunction

σοὶ δ᾽ ἐγὼ ἐνθάδε φημὶ **φόνον** καὶ **κῆρα** μέλαιναν
ἐξ ἐμέθεν τεύξεσθαι . . .

"But I say to you that **slaughter** and dark **doom**
will arise here because of me . . . " (5.652–53)

HYPERBATON: the separation of words that belong together, often to emphasize the first of the words

οὐ μὲν σοί ποτε **ἶσον** ἔχω **γέρας** ὁππότ᾽ Ἀχαιοὶ
Τρώων ἐκπέρσωσ᾽ εὖ ναιόμενον **πτολίεθρον** . . .

"I do not ever have a prize equal to yours, when the Achaeans
destroy the well-inhabited city of the Trojans . . . " (1.163–64)

HYPERBOLE: the use of exaggeration to achieve vividness

τοιοῦτοι δ᾽ εἴ πέρ μοι **ἐείκοσιν** ἀντεβόλησαν,
πάντες κ᾽ αὐτόθ᾽ ὄλοντο ἐμῷ ὑπὸ δουρὶ δαμέντες.

"But if **twenty** men of this kind met me by chance,
all would die here, killed by my spear." (16.847–48)

HYSTERON PROTERON: a reversal of the logical sequence of actions, often in order to emphasize the later action over the earlier

τοῦ περ δὴ περὶ νηὸς Ἀχαιοί τε Τρῶές τε
δήουν ἀλλήλους αὐτοσχεδόν· οὐδ᾽ ἄρα τοί γε
τόξων ἀϊκὰς ἀμφὶς μένον οὐδ᾽ ἔτ᾽ ἀκόντων . . .

"Now around his ship both Achaeans and Trojans
slew one another, hand-to-hand; then they neither
awaited the rush of bows, nor of javelins any longer . . . " (15.707–709)

LITOTES: emphasis through understatement, often achieved by negating the opposite of the desired term

ὣς ἔφαθ᾽, Ἕκτωρ δ᾽ **οὔ** τι κασιγνήτῳ **ἀπίθησεν.**

"So he spoke, and Hector **did not at all disobey** his brother." (6.102)

METAPHOR: an indirect comparison of unlikes, without the use of "like" or "as" or similar preparatory words

οὐδέ κ᾽ Ἄρης, ὅς περ θεὸς ἄμβροτος, οὐδέ κ᾽ Ἀθήνη
τοσσῆσδ᾽ ὑσμίνης ἐφέποι **στόμα** καὶ πονέοιτο·

"Neither Ares, though an immortal god, nor Athena
might work and toil **at the mouth of such a battle.**" (20.358–59)

νῦν γὰρ δὴ πάντεσσιν **ἐπὶ ξυροῦ** ἵσταται **ἀκμῆς**
ἢ μάλα λυγρὸς ὄλεθρος Ἀχαιοῖς ἠὲ βιῶναι.

"For now, indeed, it is set **on the razor's edge,**
whether mournful ruin or life, for all the Achaeans." (10.173–74)

METONYMY: a naming by the use of an associated or constituent property

> οἵ τε πανημέριοι στυγερῷ κρίνονται Ἄρηϊ
> ἄστεος ἐκ σφετέρου·

"... and all day long they are judged by hateful Ares / proved in spiteful war from their city wall ... " (18.209–10)

> πολλοὺς γὰρ Τρώων καταλείψομεν, οὕς κεν Ἀχαιοὶ
> **χαλκῷ** δηώσωσιν ἀμυνόμενοι περὶ νηῶν.

"For we shall leave behind many of the Trojans, whomever the Achaeans shall cut down with **bronze**, warding them off around the ships." (12.226–27)

ONOMATOPOEIA: a word or phrase that resembles the sound it names

> τοὺς ἔκβαλλε θύραζε **μεμυκὼς** ἠΰτε ταῦρος
> χέρσον δέ·

"**Moo**ing like a bull, he threw them out
onto the land ... " (21.237–38)

> **ἔκλαγξαν** δ᾽ ἄρ᾽ ὀϊστοὶ ἐπ᾽ ὤμων χωομένοιο,
> αὐτοῦ κινηθέντος·

"But the arrows **clanged** on his shoulders, shaking with anger
as he moved ..." (1.46–47)

OXYMORON: an apparent contradiction or illogical pairing

> δημοβόρος βασιλεύς ...

"people-devouring king ... " (1.231)

PARALLEL STRUCTURE: two or more phrases, clauses, or sentences displaying similar or parallel syntax patterns

> **ἀμφὶ δ**᾽ ἑὸν φίλον **υἱὸν ἐχεύατο** πήχεε λευκώ,
> **πρόσθε δέ οἱ** πέπλοιο φαεινοῦ πτύγμα **κάλυψεν** ...

"And around her dear son [Aphrodite] draped her white arms,
and before him she spread the fold of her gleaming robe ... " (5.314–15)

POLYSYNDETON: unnecessary use of connectors for emphasis by extenuation or for metrical fulfillment

> ἀλλ᾽ ἥ γε ξὺν παιδὶ καὶ ἀμφιπόλῳ ἐϋπέπλῳ
> πύργῳ ἐφεστήκει γοόωσά **τε** μυρομένη **τε**.

"But she with her child and her maidservant of the beautiful robe
had stood near the tower, (**both**) weeping **and** wailing." (6.372–73)

Prosopopoeia (Personification): the attribution of human appearance, quality, or emotion to an inanimate object or abstraction

ὅ δὲ Κύπριν ἐπῴχετο **νηλέϊ χαλκῷ.**

"But he attacked Aphrodite with the **pitiless** bronze." (5.330)

Ζεὺς δ' Ἔριδα προΐαλλε θοὰς ἐπὶ νῆας Ἀχαιῶν
ἀργαλέην, πολέμοιο τέρας μετὰ χερσὶν ἔχουσαν.

"And Zeus sent forth to the swift ships of the Achaeans
troublesome Strife, holding a token of war **in her hands.**" (11.3–4)

Repetition: multiple use of words or word groups to emphasize or unify an idea, often in parallel structure, including anaphora

εὖ μέν **τις** δόρυ θηξάσθω, εὖ δ' ἀσπίδα θέσθω,
εὖ **δέ τις** ἵπποισιν δεῖπνον δότω ὠκυπόδεσσιν,
εὖ **δέ τις** ἅρματος ἀμφὶς ἰδὼν πολέμοιο μεδέσθω . . .

"Let every man sharpen his spear well, and prepare his shield well,
let every man feed his swift-hooved horses well,
and let every man, knowledgable of war, be well mindful all around his chariot . . . (2.382–85)

Simile: A direct comparison featuring "like," "as," "as when," or a similar preparatory element

ὡς δ' ὅτ' ἐν αἰγιαλῷ πολυηχέϊ κῦμα θαλάσσης
ὄρνυτ' . . .
. . . ὡς τότ' ἐπασσύτεραι Δαναῶν κίνυντο φάλαγγες
νωλεμέως πόλεμον δέ·

" . . . as when a wave of the sea on the loud-echoing beach
rises . . .
. . . so then the divisions of the Danaans closer and closer stirred
the fighting without ceasing . . . " (4.422–23; 427–28)

Synchysis (Synchesis): an interwoven or "A-B-A-B" word arrangement within a line or across the line boundary

Ἕκτωρ δὲ πρυμνῆς **νεὸς** ἥψατο **ποντοπόροιο.**

"And Hector clung to the stern of a seafaring ship." (15.704)

Synecdoche: a reference to a whole achieved by using a part

ἦ καὶ **κυανέῃσιν** ἐπ' **ὀφρύσι** νεῦσε Κρονίων·

"He spoke, and the son of Cronus **nodded with his dark brow . . .** " (1.528)

Tmesis: the appearance of a verbal prefix as an independent adverb, usually to satisfy metrical constraints or to accomplish synchesis

ἦμος δ' ἠέλιος κατέδυ καὶ **ἐπὶ** κνέφας **ἦλθε** (= **ἐπῆλθε**) . . .

"But when the sun went down and darkness came on . . . " (1.475)

TOPOS: a traditional, common theme or motif; sometimes akin to a proverb

> ἀλλά με τεθνηῶτα χυτὴ κατὰ γαῖα καλύπτοι,
> πρίν γέ τι σῆς τε βοῆς σοῦ θ᾽ ἑλκηθμοῖο πυθέσθαι.

> "But may the mounded earth cover me, dead,
> before I learn anything of your wailing and of your rape."
> (6.464–65)

ZEUGMA: the use of two words in which only one carries a logical meaning

> τοὶ δὲ χάρησαν,
> ὡς εἶδον ζωόν τε καὶ ἀρτεμέα προσιόντα,
> Ἄιαντος προφυγόντα **μένος** καὶ **χεῖρας** ἀάπτους·

> "And they rejoiced
> when they saw him coming forth alive and safe,
> fleeing the **strength** and invincible **hands** of Ajax . . . " (7.307–309)

APPENDIX B

Index of Significant Names

Acamas, Trojan ally killed by **Meriones**

Achaeans, a name for the Greeks; "those from Achaea"

Achilles, son of **Peleus** and **Thetis;** his anger supplies the theme of the *Iliad*

Aeacus, father of **Peleus;** grandfather of **Achilles**

Aeneas, son of **Anchises** and **Aphrodite;** survivor of the Trojan war, later considered the ancestor of the Roman people

Agamemnon, leader of the contingent from Mycenae and of the entire Greek host at **Troy;** brother of **Menelaus**

Ajax, leader of the contingent from the island of Salamis; son of **Telamon;** cousin of **Achilles**

Ajax the Lesser, leader of the contingent from Locria; son of **Oeleus**

Alexander, see **Paris**

Amisodarus, father of **Maris** and **Atymnius**

Amphiclus, Trojan killed by **Phyleides**

Anchises, father of **Aeneas** with **Aphrodite;** descendant of **Tros**

Antilochus, son of **Nestor;** youngest Greek leader

Aphrodite, mother of **Aeneas** by **Anchises;** goddess of erotic love

Apollo, god of light, music, and plague; champion of the Trojans

Areilycus, Trojan killed by **Patroclus**

Artemis, sister of **Apollo;** archer goddess of wild places and beasts

Athena, patron warrior goddess of Athens; champion of the Greeks

Atreus, father of **Agamemnon** and **Menelaus;** former ruler of Mycenae

Atymnius, brother of Maris; Paphlagonian killed by **Antilochus**

Briseis, spear-bride of **Achilles;** captured in a raid and later seized by **Agamemnon,** leading to the withdrawal of **Achilles** from battle

Capaneus, epic hero of the previous generation; father of **Sthenelus**

Charites, the Graces

Chimaera, Lycian creature with a lion's head, a goat's body, and the tail of a snake

Chryseis, daughter of **Chryses;** spear-bride of **Agamemnon,** who refuses to ransom her until compelled by **Apollo's** plague

Chryses, priest of **Apollo;** father of **Chryseis;** invokes the plague against the Greeks

Cleobulus, Trojan killed by Oelian **Ajax**

Cronus, former ruler of the gods; father of **Zeus** and others

Cypris, Aphrodite, in association with Cyprus

Danaans, a name for the Greeks; "descendants of Danaus of Argos"

Deipylus, friend of **Sthenelus;** not mentioned elsewhere in the *Iliad*

Diomedes, leader of the contingent from Argos; son of **Tydeus**

Enyo, companion of Ares, god of war

Erebus, a name for the underworld, the dark realm

Erymas, Lycian killed by **Patroclus**

Euphorbus, wounds **Patroclus**

Ganymede, son of **Tros;** taken to Olympus by Zeus, provoking the jealousy of Hera

Hades, the underworld or its ruler

Hector, chief prince and defender of **Troy;** son of **Priam;** incites **Achilles** to return to the battlefield by killing **Patroclus**

Helen, wife of **Menelaus;** consort of **Paris**

Hephaestus, god of the forge; fashions divine armor for **Achilles**

Idomeneus, leader of the Cretan contingent

Leto, mother of **Apollo** and **Artemis** by **Zeus**

Lycaon, father of **Pandarus**

Lycaon, son of **Priam;** killed by **Achilles**

Lycon, Trojan killed by **Peneleus**

Maris, brother of Atymnius; Lycian killed by Thrasymedes

Megas, leader of the contingent from Dulichium; son of Phyleus

Menelaus, leader of the contingent from Sparta; brother of **Agamemnon;** husband of **Helen**

Menoetius, epic hero of the previous generation; father of **Patroclus**

Meriones, half-brother and charioteer of **Idomeneus**

Myrmidons, the contingent from **Phthia** led by **Achilles**

Nestor, leader of the contingent from Pylos; oldest Greek leader; epic hero of the previous generation

Odysseus, leader of the contingent from Ithaca

Oeleus, epic hero of the previous generation; father of **Ajax** the lesser

Pandarus, archer and charioteer of **Aeneas**

Paris, a prince of **Troy;** takes **Helen** as his prize after judging the fateful beauty contest among Hera, **Athena,** and **Aphrodite**

Patroclus, close friend of **Achilles;** killed in battle while wearing **Achilles'** own armor

Peleus, epic hero of the previous generation; father of **Achilles** with **Thetis**

Peneleus, leader of the contingent from Boeotia

Phoebus, epithet of **Apollo;** "shining"

Phthia, home of **Achilles** and his **Myrmidons** in north-central Greece

Plakos, mountain above the city of Thebes near **Troy**

Priam, aged king of Troy; he lives to see all his many children slain

Sarpedon, son of **Zeus;** killed by **Patroclus**

Sthenelus, leader, along with **Diomedes,** of the contingent from Argos

Telemon, epic hero of the previous generation; father of **Ajax;** brother of **Peleus**

Thetis, mother of **Achilles;** a sea-nymph desired by **Zeus,** she was married to **Peleus** after a prophecy revealed that she would bear a son who would be greater than his father

Thoas: Trojan killed by **Menelaus**

Thrasymedes, son of **Nestor**

Trojans, besieged by the Greeks after the abduction of **Helen**

Tros, eponymous ancestor of the Trojans

Troy, city near the Hellespont, on a hill now called Hissarlik in Turkey

Tydeus, epic hero of the previous generation; father of **Diomedes**

Zeus, king of gods and men

APPENDIX C

Vocabulary

ἀβληχρός, -ή, -όν, weak, soft

ἀγαθός, -ή, -όν, good

ἀγακλυτός, -όν, very famous, glorious

ἀγορή, -ῆς, ἡ, assembly

ἄγριος, -η, -ον, wild, fierce, savage

ἄγχι, near; + *gen.*, + *dat.*, near, close by

ἄγω, lead; do; drive

ἀείδω, sing

ἀέξω, increase, enlarge, strengthen

ἅζομαι, please, gratify

ἀθάνατος, -η, -ον, immortal

αἴ, = εἰ

Ἀϊδόσδε, to(ward) Hades

αἰεί, always, ever

αἰετός, -οῦ, ὁ, eagle

αἴθοψ, -οπος, shining

αἷμα, -ατος, τό, blood

ἀναίμων, ον, τό, of the gods

αἰνῶς, strongly, sharply

αἰπύς, -εῖα, -ύ, sheer, steep

αἱρέω, take hold of, seize; *in mid.*, choose

αἴτιος, -α, -ον, blameworthy

αἰχμή, -ῆς, ἡ, point

αἰχμητής, -οῦ, ὁ, spearman

αἶψα, immediately

ἀκοντίζω, hurl a javelin

ἀκοντιστής, -οῦ, ὁ, javelin thrower

ἄκρος, -η, -ον, at the tip, extremity

ἀκωκή, -ῆς, ἡ, point

ἄλγος, -εος, τό, pain, distress

ἀλεγίζω, have regard for

ἅλις, enough, sufficient

ἀλκή, -ῆς, ἡ, strength

ἄλκιμος, strong

ἀλκτήρ, -ῆρος, ὁ, defender

ἀλλά, but

ἀλλήλων, one another

ἄλλος, -η, -ο, (an)other

ἀλύω, be distressed

ἅμα, + *dat.*, together with

ἀμαιμάκετος, -η, -ον, huge

ἀμαλός, -ή, -όν, tender, gentle; feeble

ἁμαρτάνω, miss, fail to hit, + *gen.*

ἀμβατός, -όν, capable of being scaled

ἀμβρόσιος, -ον, immortal, divine

ἄμβροτος, -ον, immortal, divine

ἀμείβω, reply; exchange

ἀμείνων, -ον, better

ἀμολγός, -οῦ, ὁ, gloom, darkness

ἀμύμων, -ονος, blameless, excellent

ἀμφί, around, over; + *dat.*, + *acc.*, around, about

ἀμφικαλύπτω, cover on both sides, cover completely

ἄμφω, both

ἄν, untranslatable particle used with some conditions and to show potentiality

ἀνά, + *dat.*, on, along; + *acc.*, throughout

ἀνάγκη, -ης, ἡ, necessity

ἀναιδείη, -ης, ἡ, shamelessness

ἄναλκις, -ιδος, incapable of defense; unsuited for battle

ἄναξ, -ακτος, ὁ, lord, ruler

ἀνάσσω, rule over

ἀνδρότης, -ητος, ὁ, courage, manliness

ἀνήρ, ἀνδρός, ὁ, man; husband

ἄνθρωπος, -ου, ὁ / ἡ, person

ἀντάξιος, -ον, worth an equal amount

ἄντην, face to face, openly against

ἀντιβολέω, meet, encounter

ἀντίθεος, -ον, godlike

ἀντικρύ, straight through

ἀντίος, -η, -ον, opposite, against

ἀντιτορέω, pierce, + *gen.*

ἄντυξ, -υγος, ἡ, front rail of a chariot; shield rim

ἀνώγω, command, order, bid

ἀπαλός, -ή, -όν, tender, soft

ἀπαμείβω, *in mid.*, answer, reply

ἀπαράσσω, smash

ἀπειλέω, declare, promise

ἀπερείσιος, -ον, boundless

ἀπό, away, away from, back; + *gen.*, from, away from

ἀποβαίνω, go away

ἀποδίδωμι, give away, give back

ἄποινα, -ων, τά, ransom

ἀπολάμπω, shine forth

ἀπόλλυμι, kill, destroy; *in mid.*, be destroyed, perish

ἀπολύω, untie, set free

ἀπορέω, be at a loss

ἀπορούω, spring, dart off

ἀποτίνω, pay back

ἄρ / ἄρα, *expresses consequence or sequence*, and so, then

ἀραρίσκω, join; fit close

ἀράσσω, break, smash

ἀργεννός, -ή -όν, white

ἀργύρεος, -η, -ον, made of silver

ἀργυρόηλος, -ον, with silver nails

ἀρή, -ῆς, ἡ, harm, ruin
ἀρήϊος, -ον, warlike
ἀρητήρ, -ῆρος, ὁ, priest
ἄριστος, -η, -ον, best
ἁρμόζω, fit, adjust; *in mid.*, fit well
ἀρνός, -έος, ὁ / ἡ, lamb
ἄρνυμαι, earn, win
ἄρουρα, -ης, ἡ, farmland, good earth
ἁρπάζω, seize
ἄρτιος, -ον, suitable
ἀσπίς, -ίδος, ἡ, shield
ἀστήρ, -έρος, ὁ, star
ἀσφάραγος, -ου, ὁ, wind-pipe
ἀτάρ, see αὐτάρ
ἀτιμάζω, dishonor
αὖ, again, in turn
αὖθι, right there; right then
αὐτάρ, but
αὐτίκα, immediately
αὖτις, again; in reverse
αὐτόθι, on the spot; immediately
αὐτός, -ή, -ό, him / her / it; *in nom. always intensive of subj.* (-self)
αὐτοσχεδά, from near by
αὐτοῦ, there, in that place
αὔτως, so, in this way; merely, in vain
αὐχήν, -ένος, ὁ, neck
ἀΰω, shout, cry out
ἀφαιρέω, take away
ἀφαμαρτάνω, miss, fail to hit
ἄφαρ, quickly
ἀφραδίη, -ης, ἡ, senselessness, recklessness
ἄχθος, -εος, -τό, burden, weight
ἀχλύς, -ύος, ἡ, mist
ἄχνυμαι, be grieved, be troubled
ἄχρις, utterly, completely
ἄψ, again; back, backward

βαίνω, go
βάλλω, throw; hit, strike
βασιλεύς, -ῆος, ὁ, king
βασιλεύω, rule
βείομαι, live
βέλος, -εος, τό, missile
βίη, -ης, ἡ, force
βλάπτω, catch, impede
βοή, -ῆς, ἡ, shout
βουκολέω, tend cattle
βουλή, -ῆς, ἡ, plan; council of chiefs
βοῦς, βοός, ὁ / ἡ, cattle
βραχίων, -ονος, ὁ, arm
βροτός, -οῦ, ὁ / ἡ, mortal
βωτιάνειρα, *fem.,* man-feeding

γαῖα, -ας, ἡ, earth
γάρ, for, for indeed
γε, *particle stressing preceding word,* at least, certainly
γεν-, *aor. stem* < γίγνομαι
γέρας, -αος, τό, prize of honor
γίγνομαι, become
γιγνώσκω, know
γλαφυρός, -ή, -όν, hollow
γλυκίος, -α, -ον, sweet
γνύξ, on bended knee
γοάω, weep, wail, + *acc.*
γυῖα, -ων, τά, limbs
γυμνόω, strip; *in pass.,* laid bare
γυνή, γυναικός, ἡ, woman; wife

δαιδάλεος, -η, -ον, carefully made
δαμάζω, conquer, master, subdue
δέ, but; and
δείδω, fear
δεινός, -ή, -όν, terrible, dreadful
δεξιός, -ά, -όν, on the right side
δεξιτερός, -ά, -όν, right-handed
δέρμα, -ατος, τό, skin
δεῦρο, to here, hither
δεύτερος, -α, -ον, second
δεύω / δεύομαι, lack, want
δέχομαι, accept, receive
δέω, lack, be in need of, + *gen.*

δή, *temporal particle,* now, already; *emphatic particle,* of course
δηϊοτής, -ῆτος, ἡ, battle
δηλέομαι, do harm
δηρός, -ή, -όν, *of time,* long
διά, through; + *gen.,* through; + *acc.,* passing through; on account of
διαπρό, straight through
διαρπάζω, seize and tear to pieces
διασχίζω, sever, tear
διατμήγω, divide in two, sever
δίδωμι, give, grant
διελαύνω, drive through
διΐστημι, stand apart
δῖος, -α, -ον, shining, brilliant
διοτρεφής, -ές, cherished by Zeus
δοιοί, -αί, -ά, two, double
δοκεύω, watch closely
δόρυ, δουρός, τό, spear
δουπέω, clatter, fall with a noise
δρύπτω, strip, tear
δύνω, = δύω
δυσκέλαδος, -ον, full of cries
δύω / δύο, two
δύω, sink; get into, put on
δῶμα, -ατος, τό, house, hall

ἐάω, allow
ἐγκέφαλος, -η, -ον, brain
ἔγνων, *aor.* < γιγνώσκω
ἔγχος, -εος, τό, spear
ἐγώ, μου / μοῦ, I
ἔγωγε, *emphatic,* < ἐγώ
ἔδω, eat
ἔθειραι, -ων, αἱ, horse-hair; plume of a helmet
ἐθέλω, be willing; wish
εἰ, if; whether
εἰ μή, if . . . not; unless
εἶδον, *aor.* < ὁράω
εἶθαρ, immediately
εἴκοσι(ν), *indeclinable,* twenty
εἴκω,[1] *impersonal,* seem likely

εἴκω,[2] *of fighting*, yield; withdraw from, + *gen.*

εἰλίπους, -ποδος, with rolling gait

εἷλον, *aor.* < αἱρέω

εἴλω, crowd together, hem in, shut up

εἰμί, be

εἶμι, go

εἵνεκα, = ἕνεκα

εἶπον, *aor.* < λέγω

εἰσοράω, look upon, look closely at

ἐΐσος, -η, -ον, well-balanced

εἴσω, in; + *acc.*, + *gen.*, into, within

ἐκ, from, out; + *gen.*, out of; from

ἕκαστος, -η, -ον, each

ἑκηβόλος, -ον, far darter, far shooter

ἐκπεράω, pass through

ἐκπέρθω, sack thoroughly; + *gen.*, pillage from

ἑλ-, *aor. stem* < αἱρέω

ἔλαβον, *aor.* < λαμβάνω

ἔλαθον, *aor.* < λανθάνω

ἐλαύνω, drive, impel; strike

ἐλεαίρω, pity

ἐλθ-, *aor. stem* < ἔρχομαι

ἕλωρ, ——, τό, prey, spoil

ἐμμεμαώς, υῖα, ός, eager

ἐμός, -ή, -όν, my

ἐμπίπλημι, fill

ἐν, + *dat.*, in

ἐναρίζω, strip, despoil

ἕνεκα, + *preceding gen.*, on account of

ἔνθα, there, where; then

ἐνί, = ἐν

ἐννέπω, say, tell

ἐνστρέφω, turn inside of

ἔντεα, -ων, τά, armor

ἐντός, within

ἐξ, = ἐκ

ἐξαλαπάζω, destroy, sack

ἐξελαύνω, drive forth; march

ἐξεναρίζω, strip of armor; slay

ἐξέπραθον, *aor.* < ἐκπέρθω

ἑός, -ή, -όν, his / her / its own

ἐπαγείρω, collect together

ἐπαΐσσω, rush at

ἐπαμύνω, defend, rescue

ἐπεί, when; since, because

ἔπειτα, then, next

ἐπέοικε, be fit, suitable for

ἐπεύχομαι, boast over

ἐπί, to(ward); + *gen.*, upon; + *dat.*, on, upon, at; + *acc.*, to(ward)

ἐπιβαίνω, set foot upon; *of horses*, mount, + *gen.*

ἐπίδρομος, -ον, easily overrun

ἐπιέννυμι, be clothed in

ἐπινεύω, nod

ἐπισσεύω, set upon; *in pass.*, be eager, be incited

ἐπισφυρία, -ων, τά, bands, clasps for greaves

ἐπιτέλλω, enjoin, charge, command

ἐπιχράω, attack, + *dat.*

ἐποίχομαι, go against

ἕπομαι, follow

ἐπορέγω, *in mid.*, reach out to strike

ἐπορούω, rush at, + *dat.*

ἔπος, -εος, τό, word

ἐποτρύνω, stir to action, incite, urge

ἑπτά, *indeclinable*, seven

ἔργον, -ου, τό, deed

ἐρεβεννός, -ή, -όν, dark

ἐρείδω, prop up, push; *in mid.*, lean, + *gen.*

ἐρείπω, throw down; *aor.*, fall

ἐρέω, *fut.*, tell, say

ἐριβῶλαξ, -ακος, fertile

ἐρίζω, quarrel

ἐρινεός, -οῦ, ὁ, wild fig tree

ἔρις, -ιδος, ἡ, strife

ἔριφος, -ου, ὁ, young goat, kid

ἕρκος, -εος, τό, barrier

ἐρύκω, hold back

ἐρύω, draw, pull

ἔρχομαι, go, come

ἐς, + *acc.*, toward, into

ἐσθλός, -ή, -όν, noble

ἕσπερος, -ου, ὁ, evening

ἔσχον, *aor.* < ἔχω

ἑταῖρος, -ου, ὁ, companion

ἑτάρος, -ου, ὁ, see ἑταῖρος

ἑτέρωθι, from elsewhere

ἐτώσιος, -ον, vain, worthless

εὖ / ἐΰ, well

εὐήκης, -ες, sharp-pointed

ἐϋκνήμις, -ιδος, well-greaved

εὐτείχεος, -ον, well-walled

εὔτυκτος, -ον, well made

εὔχομαι, boast; pray

ἐφίημι, incite; *in mid.*, lay an injunction upon

ἐφορμάω, stir to action, incite; *mid. / pass.*, rush upon; be eager

ἐχθρός, -ή, -όν, hateful to, + *dat.*

ἔχω, have, hold

ζωός, -ή, -όν, alive, living

ἤ, or

ἢ . . . ἤ, either . . . or

ἦ, *affirmative particle*, indeed, truly

ᾗ, (in the place) where

ἥβη, -ης, ἡ, youth

ἤγαγον, *aor.* < ἄγω

ἡγεμών, -όνος, ὁ, leader

ἠδέ, and

ἠδὲ . . . ἠμέν, both . . . and

ἤδη, already, by now, before this

ἦλθον, *aor.* < ἔρχομαι

ἦμαι, sit; sit idle

ἦμαρ, -ατος, τό, day

ἡμεῖς, ἡμῶν, *pl.* < ἐγώ

ἠμέν, see ἠδέ

ἡνία, -ων, τά, reins

ἠπεροπεύω, deceive, lead astray

ἥρως, -ωος, ὁ, hero

ἠΰκομος, -ον, with beautiful hair

ἠΰτε, *introduces a simile*, as; as when

ἠχήεις, -εσσα, -εν, echoing

θάλασσα, -ης, ἡ, sea

θαλερός, -ή, -όν, blooming, fresh

θαμέες, θαμειαί, pl., set close together, thick; frequent

θάνατος, -ου, ὁ, death

θείνω, strike

θέναρ, -αρος, τό, palm of the hand

θεοείκελος, -ον, like a god, god-like

θεοπρόπιον, -ου, τό, omen, oracle

θεός, -οῦ, ὁ / ἡ, god

θην, affirmative particle, often with ironic force

θλάω, smash, crush

θνήσκω, die, be killed

θοός, -ή, -όν, swift

θοῦρις, -ιδος, impetuous, furious

θυγάτηρ, -τρός, ἡ, daughter

θυμός, -οῦ, ὁ, spirit; bravery

θώρηξ, -ηκος, ὁ, breastplate

ἰάχω, shout

ἰδ-, aor. stem < ὁράω

ἵημι, let go, hurl; put to

ἱκ-, aor. stem < ἱκνέομαι

ἱκνέομαι, arrive, reach

ἵνα, where; so that, + subjnc.

ἰός, -ή, -όν, one, single

ἰός, -οῦ, ὁ, arrow

ἰοχέαιρα, fem. only, shedder of arrows

ἱππεύς, -ῆος, ὁ, chariot-fighter

ἱππόκομος, -ον, with horse-hair crest

ἵππος, -ου, ὁ / ἡ, horse

ἵππουρις, -ιδος, crested with horse hair

ἴσος, -η, -ον, equal to, + dat.

ἵστημι, stand

ἴσχιον, -ου, τό, hip socket

ἴφθιμος, -ον, strong, brave

ἶφι, strongly

ἰχώρ, -ῶρος, ὁ, fluid in gods' veins

καθύπερθε(ν), from above

καί, and; also, as well; even

καίπερ, although, + pple.

κακός, -ή, -όν, bad, wicked, base

καλέω, call

καλλίθριξ, -τριχος, with beautiful hair

καλλιπάρῃος, -ον, fair-cheeked

καλός, -ή, -όν, fine, beautiful

καλύπτω, conceal, enfold; draw as cover over

κάμω, make; do

καπνός, -οῦ, ὁ, smoke

κάρη, κάρητος / κρατός, τό, head

καρπάλιμος, -ον, swift

καρπός, -οῦ, ὁ, fruit, crop

καρτερός, -ή, -όν, strong, powerful

κασίγνητος, -ου, ὁ, brother

κατά, + gen., down from; down over; + acc., down along; according to; in respect to

καταβάλλω, throw down, drop

κατακτείνω, kill, slay

καταλείβω, drip down

καταπίπτω, fall down

καταφένω, kill, slay

κατεπέφνον, aor. only, kill, slay

καυλός, -οῦ, ὁ, spear shaft; sword hilt

κε = ἄν; with fut. may indicate conditionality

κεάζω, split, cleave

κεδάννυμι, scatter, disperse

κεῖμαι, lie, be placed

κελαινός, -ή, -όν, dark, black

κέλομαι, command, bid

κεν = κε

κερδαλεόφρων, -ονος, greedy

κεφαλή, -ῆς, ἡ, head

κήρ, κηρός, ὁ, fate, death

κῆρ, κῆρος, τό, heart

κιχάνω, overtake, reach

κίω, go, come

κλέπτω, steal; deceive

κλῆΐς, -ῖδος, ἡ, bolt; clavicle, collar bone

κλισίηνδε, to(ward) the tent

κλόνος, -ου, ὁ, confusion, panic

κνήμη, -ης, ἡ, lower leg

κνημίς, -ίδος, ἡ, greaves

κοίρανέω, rule over

κοίρανος, -ου, ὁ, leader

κονίη, -ης, ἡ, dust

κόρυς, -υθος, ὁ, helmet

κοσμήτωρ, -ορος, ὁ, leader

κοτέω, resent, be angry at

κοτύλη, -ης, ἡ, cup; socket

κούρη, -ης, ἡ, girl

κραταιός, -ή, -όν, strong, powerful

κρατερῶνυξ, -υχος, strong-hoofed

κρείων, -ον, stronger; as epithet, ruler

κτέαρ, -ατος, τό, possession

κτείνω, kill

κυάνεος, -η, -ον, deep blue, dark

κύδιστος, -η, -ον, most praised

κυνέη, -ης, ἡ, helmet

κυνῶπις, -ιδος, dog-eyed

κύων, κυνός, ὁ / ἡ, dog

κωπήεις, -εσσα, -εν, hilted; with a handle

λαβ-, aor. stem < λαμβάνω

λαγωός, ὁ / ἡ, hare

λαθ-, aor. stem < λανθάνω

λαμβάνω, take, seize

λανθάνω, escape notice; in mid., forget

λαός, -οῦ, ὁ, people; troops

λαπάρη, -ης, ἡ, hollow under the ribs, flank

λαυκανίη, -ης, ἡ, throat

λέγω, say

λείπω, leave, leave behind

λευκός, -ή, -όν, white

λέων, -οντος, ὁ, lion

λίθος, -ου, ὁ, stone

λίσσομαι, beg
λόφος, -ου, ὁ, crest
λύκος, -ου, ὁ, wolf
λύω, loosen, set free; dissolve

μάκαρ, -αρος, blessed
μακρός, -ή, -όν, long
μάλα, especially, very; by all
    means
μάλιστα, especially, most of all
μαντεύω, prophesy
μάχη, -ης, ἡ, battle
μάχομαι, fight
μεγάθυμος, -ον, great-hearted
μέγαρον, -ου, τό, house, hall
μέγας, μεγάλη, μέγα, large,
    great
μεθάλλομαι, spring at, rush
    upon
μεθέπω, follow
μέλας, μέλαινα, μέλαν, black,
    dark
μέλεος, -η, -ον, vain, useless,
    empty
μέλι, -ιτος, τό, honey
μελίη, -ης, ἡ, ash spear
μέλλω, be about (to); impf., be
    destined (to)
μέμαα, pf. only, be eager, contend
μέν, indeed, certainly
μέν . . . δέ, coordinating particles,
    on one hand . . . on the other
    hand
μένος, -εος, τό, spirit, might
μένω, remain; await
μετά, among, with; + gen., with;
    + dat., among; + acc., after;
    among
μεταξύ, in between
μετατρέπομαι, care for, be con-
    cerned about
μή, not
μῆλον, -ου, τό, sheep, goats
μῆνις, -ιος, ἡ, wrath, ire
μηρός, -οῦ, ὁ, thigh
μήτηρ, -τρός, ἡ, mother
μητίετα, ὁ, counselor, deviser

μιμνήσκω, remind; in mid.,
    remember, call to mind
μίμνω, remain
μιν, acc., him; her
μοῖρα, -ης, ἡ, fate, doom
μυρίος, -η, -ον, ten thousand;
    countless
μυών, -ῶνος, ὁ, muscle
μῶνυξ, -υχος, single hoofed

νεκρός, -οῦ, ὁ, corpse
νέκυς, -υος, ὁ, corpse
νέομαι, go, come; return
νέρθεν, beneath, below
νεῦρα, -ων, τά, nerves
νεύω, nod
νεφέλη, -ης, ἡ, cloud, mist
νέφος, -εος, τό, cloud, mist
νίκη, -ης, ἡ, victory
νηλεής, -ές, pitiless
νηῦς, -ός, ἡ, ship
νοέω, understand; notice
νόος, -ου, ὁ, mind
νόσφι(ν), far from, separate from
νοῦσος, -ου, ἡ, disease, sickness
νυ / νυν, emphatic particle, now
    indeed
νῦν, now
νύξ, νυκτός, ἡ, night
νύσσω, wound, pierce; thrust

ξίφος, -εος, τό, sword
ξυνήϊος, -ον, common; in pl.,
    common property
ξυνίημι, see συνίημι

ὁ, ἡ, τό, the; that, those, = αὐτός,
    -ή, -ό
ὅδε, ἥδε, τόδε, this
ὁδός, -οῦ, ἡ, road
ὀδών, -όντος, ὁ, tooth
ὄθομαι, care for, pay heed
οἶδα, know
οἴκαδε, to(ward) home
οἰμάω, spring upon
οἶνος, -ου, ὁ, wine

οἶος, -η, -ον, alone, only
οἷος, -η, -ον, as, of which sort
ὄϊς, ὄϊός, ὁ / ἡ, sheep
ὀΐω, think
οἰωνός, -οῦ, ὁ, bird
ὄλεθρος, -ου, ὁ, destruction,
    death
ὀλέκω, destroy, kill; in pass., die
ὀλετήρ, -ῆρος, ὁ, destroyer,
    slayer
ὀλιγοδρανέων, pple. only, pow-
    erless, weak
ὄλλυμι, destroy, kill
ὀλοός, -ή, -όν, destructive, bane-
    ful
Ὀλύμπιος, -η, -ον, Olympian,
    on Mt. Olympus
ὁμηλικίη, -ης, ὁ, age-mate, of
    the same age
ὅμιλος, -ου, ὁ, crowd
ὁμοιόω, liken; vie with
ὀξυόεις, -εσσα, -εν, sharp,
    pointed
ὀξύς, -εῖα, -ύ, sharp
ὀπάζω, joining, pressing upon
ὅπη, where; wherever
ὁππότε, when(ever)
ὅπως, so that
ὁράω, see
ὀρέγω, stretch; in mid., reach; hit
ὁρμάω, set in motion, impel
ὄρνυμι, stir up
ὄρος, -εος, τό, mountain
ὀρφανικός, -όν, fatherless
ὅς, ἥ, ὅ, who, which, that
ὄσσε, dual, eyes
ὅσσος, -η, -ον, how much; as
    much as
ὀστέον, -ου, τό, bone
ὅτε, when
ὅτι, that; because
οὔας, -ατος, τό, ear; handle of
    a cup
οὐδέ, and . . . not; not even
οὐλόμενος, -η, -ον, destroying,
    destructive
οὐρανός, -οῦ, ὁ, heaven

οὖρος, -ου, ὁ, protector

οὐτάω, wound; strike

οὔτε, *correlated with negative clause*, neither . . . (nor)

οὗτος, αὕτη, τοῦτο, this, that

οὕτως, thus, in this way

ὀφθαλμός, -οῦ, ὁ, eye

ὄφρα, until, so long as; + *subjnc.*, (in order) that

ὄχεα, -ων, τά, *pl.*, chariot

ὀχέω, hold fast, endure; be carried

ὀχθέω, be troubled, be angry

παῖς, παιδός, ὁ / ἡ, child

παλάμη, -ης, ἡ, hand

παλάμηφι(ν), in the hand

παλίλλογος, -ον, gathered up again

πάλλω, shake, brandish; hurl

πάντοσε, in all directions

πάρ, beside, by, near

παρά, + *dat.*, beside, by; + *acc.*, to the side of, alongside

παραείρω, detach; *in pass.*, hang down on one side

παρακοίτης, -ου, ὁ, bed-mate

πάρειμι, be present

παρελαύνω, march past

παρέρχομαι, pass by, go past; outwit

παρίστημι, take up a position, stand alongside

πᾶς, πᾶσα, πᾶν, all; every; whole, entire

πατήρ, -τρός, ὁ, father

πάτρη, -ης, ἡ, fatherland; home

πατρίς, -ίδος, ἡ, homeland

παχύς, -εῖα, -ύ, thick, stout; clotted

πεδίονδε, to earth

πείθω, persuade; *in mid.*, obey

πειράω, try

πέλομαι, be; become

πέμπω, send

πέπλος, -ου, ὁ, robe

περ, *intensive particle*, indeed; *concessive particle*, although

περί, around, round about; + *gen.*, about; beyond; + *dat.*, around, about

περισσείω, wave about

πεσ-, *aor. stem* < πίπτω

πέτομαι, fly

πῆχυς, -εος, ὁ, forearm

πίμπλημι, fill

πίνω, drink

πίπτω, fall

πλήσσω, strike

ποδάρκης, -ες, swift-footed

ποθι, somewhere; ever

ποιμήν, -ένος, ὁ, shepherd

πόλεμος, -ου, ὁ, war

πόλις, -ιος / -ηος, ἡ, city

πολύς, πολλή, πολύ, much, many; great

πολύφρων, -ονος, very wise, mindful

πορφύρεος, -η, -ον, purple; gushing

πόσις, -ιος, ὁ, husband

πόσις, -ιος, ἡ, drink

πότε, when?

ποτε, ever

ποτμός, -οῦ, ὁ, fate, doom

πότνια, -ας, ἡ, mistress; *as epithet*, revered

που, where?

που, somewhere; somehow

πούς, πόδος, ὁ, foot

πρήθω, spout; blow

πρηνής, -ές, prone; falling headlong

πρίν, before; until

προϊάπτω, throw

προΐημι, let go; surrender

προπάροιθε, in front of; forward

πρός, + *gen.*, from; + *dat.*, in opposition; + *acc.*, toward

προσαυδάω, speak to, accost

προσεῖπον, spoke to, addressed

προσέφη, *aor.* < πρόσφημι

πρόσθε(ν), before; + *gen.*, before, in front of

πρόσφημι, address, speak to

προτεύχω, let go forth, let pass

προτι-, = προσ-

πρόφρων, -ονος, kindly, willing(ly); earnest(ly)

πρυμνός, -ή, -όν, hindmost part; base

πρῶτος, -η, -ον, first

πτολίπορθος, -ον, sacker of cities

πτύγμα, -ατος, τό, folds of clothing

πτώξ, -ωκός, ὁ, cowering, timid; hare

πυνθάνομαι, learn by inquiry

πύργος, -ου, ὁ, tower

πω, yet

πωλέομαι, go into

πωλέω, sell

πῶς, how?

πως, somehow

ῥα, = ἄρα

ῥαίω, shatter, break in pieces

ῥέα, easily

ῥέθεα, -ων, τά, limbs

ῥέω, flow

ῥήγνυμι, break

ῥηϊδίως, easily

ῥιγέω, shudder at

ῥινόν, -οῦ, τό, skin, hide

ῥίς, ῥινός, ἡ, nose

σάκος, -εος, τό, shield

σέθεν, *gen.* < σύ

σιγαλόεις, -εσσα, -εν, shining, glistening

σίντης, -ου, ravening

σῖτος, -ου, ὁ, grain; bread

σκέλος, -ου, τό, leg

σκῆπτρον, -ου, τό, scepter

σκιόεις, -εσσα, -εν, shaded, shadowy

σκότος, -ου, ὁ, darkness

σμερδαλέα, loudly

σός, -ή, -όν, your

στέμμα, -ατος, τό, wreath, ribbon

στέρνον, -ου, τό, chest

στῆθος, -εος, τό, chest

στιβαρός, -ή, -όν, heavy, stout

στόμα, -ατος, τό, mouth

στρατός, -οῦ, ὁ, army

στρέφω, turn, bend; *in mid. / pass.*, turn round

στυγέω, dread; hesitate

σύ, σου / σοῦ, you

σύν, + *dat.*, with

συνθεσίη, -ης, ἡ, covenant, instructions

συνίημι, send together

συντρέχω, rush together

σφεῖς, σφῶν, they

σφωε, the two

ταχύπωλος, -ον, with swift horses

τε, and, also

    τε καί, both . . . and

    τε . . . τε, both . . . and

τείνω, stretch, strain

τείρομαι, wear down

τεῖχος, -εος, τό, wall

τελέω / τελείω, accomplish, fulfill

τέλος, -εος, τό, end

τέμνω, cut

τένων, -οντος, ὁ, tendon

τέος, -η, -ον, your (*sg.*)

τετραπλόος, -η, -ον, fourfold

τετραφάλος, -ον, with four plumes

τεύχεα, -ων, τά, armor, array

τεύχω, make, prepare; *in pass.*, be, become

τηλόθι, + *gen.*, far away from

τίθημι, put, place

τίκτω, bear (a child)

τιμάω, honor

τιμή, -ῆς, ἡ, honor

τινάσσω, shake, brandish

τις, τι, someone, something

    τι, at all

τίς, τί, who? what?

    τί, why?

τίω, honor (*variant of* τίνω)

τοι, indeed; (I say) to you; your

τοῖος, -η, -ον, such a sort

τοιοῦτος, -η, -ον, such a sort

τόσος, -η, -ον, as many as

τότε, then, at that time

τοῦ, there, in that place

τρέφω, nourish, raise

τρηχύς, -εῖα, -ύ, rough

τριπλόος, -η, -ον, threefold

τρίς, thrice

τρίτος, -η, -ον, third

τύπτω, strike, beat

τῶ / τώ, therefore, so

τῷ therefore, so

υἱός, -οῦ, ὁ, son

ὑληέσσος, -η, -ον, wooded

ὑμεῖς, ὑμῶν, *pl.* < σύ

ὑπέκ, + *gen.*, out from under

ὑπεκφέρω, carry away from, + *gen.*

ὑπέρ / ὕπερ + *gen.*, above, on behalf of; + *acc.*, beyond

ὑπό, + *gen.*, from under; by; + *dat.*, under; by the agency of; + *acc.*, towards below

ὑπόδρα, with a scowl

ὑποθερμαίνω, *aor. pass.*, become heated

ὑπολύω, loose from under, undo

ὑσμίνη, -ης, ἡ, combat; battle-line

ὑψιπετήεις, -εσσα, -εν, high-flying

φαεινός, -ή, -όν, shining

φαίδιμος, -η, -ον, brilliant, bright

φαίνομαι, appear, seem

φάλος, -ου, ὁ, helmet device bearing a plume

φάος, -ου, ὁ, light

φάσγανον, -ου, τό, sword

φέρτερος, -η, -ον, stronger

φέρω, carry, bear

φεύγω, flee

φημί, say, claim

φθάνω, be first, anticipate

φθίω, waste away, perish

φιλοκτέανος, -ον, greedy

φίλος, -η, -ον, (own) dear; own

φλοῖσβος, -ου, ὁ, noise of battle; crashing of waves

φόβος, -ου, ὁ, fear

φρήν, φρενός, ἡ, mind, seat of intelligence

φρονέω, think; understand

φωνέω, speak

χαίρω, greet, be delighted

χαλεπαίνω, act in rage

χάλκεος, -ον, made of bronze

χαλκοβαρής, -ές, weighted with bronze

χαλκός, -οῦ, ὁ, bronze

χαλκοχίτων, -ωνος, bronze-clad

χάσκω, cause to gape

χεῖρ, χειρός, ἡ, hand

χερμάδιον, -ου, τό, large stone

χέω, pour, shed; heap up

χήρη, -ης, ἡ, widow

χόλος, -ου, ὁ, anger

χολόω, enrage; *in mid. / pass.*, be angry

χρῆμα, -ατος, τό, thing; possession

χρύσεος, -η, -ον, golden

χρώς, χροός / χρωτός, ὁ, flesh, skin

ψυχή, -ῆς, ἡ, soul, spirit; life

ὦ, O, Oh

ὧδε, thus, in this way

ὠθέω, push, thrust

ὠκύς, -εῖα, -ύ, swift

ὦμος, -ου, ὁ, shoulder

ὦρσα, *aor.* < ὄρνυμι

ὥς, thus, in this way

ὡς / ὧς, just as, just so; since

ὦσα, *aor.* < ὠθέω

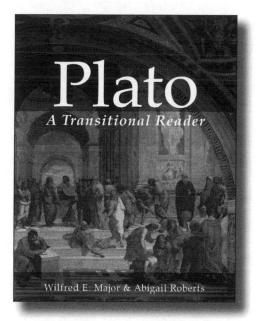

Plato
A Transitional Reader

Wilfred E. Major and Abigail Roberts

Student Text: xx + 108 pp. (2010) Paperback, ISBN 978-0-86516-721-6
Teacher's Guide: ix + 78 pp. (2012) Paperback, ISBN 978-0-86516-779-7

This graded reader helps students make the transition from beginning instruction in Greek to reading unaltered texts of Plato. It features six Greek passages: four extracts from the Republic, the summary of the *Republic* in the *Timaeus*, and the beginning of the *Euthyphro*, which sets the scene for the *Apology*. Each passage is presented in multiple versions, beginning with a very basic outline and culminating in the passage as Plato wrote it. Passages are accompanied by facing vocabulary and notes. Each unit includes a review of grammar crucial for the passage. Appendices provide two vocabulary lists that help students identify which words to memorize first.

Students completing this reader will be prepared to read full Platonic dialogues in unadapted Greek.

Features:

- Introduction to Plato with starter bibliography
- Greek texts with each passage presented in graded stages
- Facing notes and vocabulary
- Grammar reviews
- Three appendices:
    - Guide to dialogues of Plato
    - Fifty most common words in Plato
    - Five hundred most common words in Plato
- Map of Athens

Wilfred E. Major is an Assistant Professor of Classics at Louisiana State University. He works on Greek pedagogy, especially improved curricula for beginning and intermediate classes. He also conducts scurrilous research into ancient Greek Comedy.

Abigail Roberts teaches Latin and Greek at McCallie School in Chattanooga, Tennessee. When not conjugating verbs, she enjoys outdoor sports and working in the garden.

 BOLCHAZY-CARDUCCI PUBLISHERS, INC.
WWW.BOLCHAZY.COM

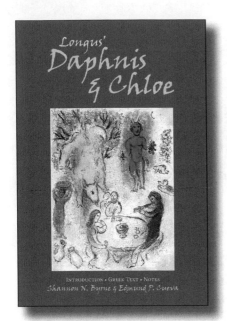

Longus'
Daphnis & Chloe
GREEK TEXT • NOTES • VOCABULARY
Shannon N. Byrne & Edmund P. Cueva

xvi + 350 pp. (2005) 6" x 9" Paperback, ISBN 978-0-86516-593-9

Longus' *Daphnis and Chloe* is a delightful tale of young love and country life that stands on its own, without needing background information. Longus' Greek is straightforward and provides ample opportunity for review of Attic Greek, while the running glossary and notes move the reading along.

Designed for intermediate classroom use, this new edition of a much-loved text includes a thorough introduction to the personal and literary context. The Greek text is accompanied by comprehensive vocabulary notes and extensive commentary.

This edition features

- Introduction to Longus' life
- Background to the ancient novel
- Running vocabulary with parallel Greek text and commentary
- Up-to-date select bibliography
- Index deorum and Index nominum
- Full glossary

Shannon N. Byrne and **Edmund P. Cueva** are coauthors of *Veritatis Amicitiaeque Causa* (1999) and *Humor and Classical Literature* (2001), and are editors of *The Classical Bulletin*. Edmund P. Cueva is also the author of *The Myths of Fiction: Studies in the Canonical Greek Novels* (2004). He holds a PhD in Classics from Loyola University, Chicago, and is Chair and Professor of Arts & Humanities at University of Houston–Downtown. Shannon N. Byrne holds a PhD in Classics from Northwestern University and is Chair and Associate Professor of Classics at Xavier University, Cincinnati.

  **BOLCHAZY-CARDUCCI PUBLISHERS, INC.**
WWW.BOLCHAZY.COM